Angels Flight: A History of Bunker Hill's Incline Railway
by Virginia L. Comer is the first in a series of publications by the Historical Society of Southern California
celebrating the Sesquicentennial of California, 1846-1850.

ANGELS FLIGHT:

A History of Bunker Hill's Incline Railway

DEDICATION

To Leo Politi, artist and author, whose graceful art has preserved historic scenes of Angels Flight and Bunker Hill and imbued them with the richness of his own spirit, this book is dedicated with esteem.

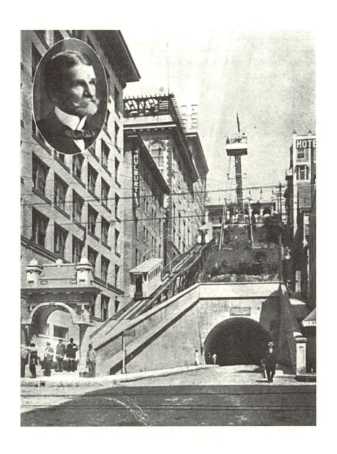

ANGELS FLIGHT:
A History of Bunker Hill's
Incline Railway

Virginia L. Comer

Historical Society of Southern California
Los Angeles 1996

Grants from the Spring Street Foundation
and the Thomas F. Andrews Fund for History,
established by members of the Historical Society,
have underwritten this publication. In addition, a grant
from the ARCO Foundation has made possible the
distribution of this book to the schools in Los Angeles
County. The Historical Society of Southern California
is pleased to acknowledge with appreciation
this generous support.

Designed by Margaret Yasuda
Cover art by Joseph Stoddard
Drawings by Ilma Cunningham

Printed in the United States of America

FOREWORD

The media coverage given to the Re-Dedication and Re-Opening of Angels Flight in downtown Los Angeles in February 1996 documents the fact that historic nostalgia for things past is alive and well. Print media attention was reinforced by the visual media in respect to TV coverage, culminating in a two-hour PBS documentary. The world's shortest funicular railroad has become a hit for the curious and a lure for history buffs. Such enthusiasm can now be reinforced by this engaging history of Angels Flight authored by Virginia L. Comer.

Ms. Comer is one of Southern California's outstanding local historians, one who has an affectionate regard for the City of the Angels. This is attested to in her previously published books, *Los Angeles: A View From Crown Hill* (1986) and *In Victorian Los Angeles, The Witmers of Crown Hill* (1988). The Crown Hill area of the city lies roughly between Union Avenue on the west, Beverly Boulevard on the north, the Harbor Freeway on the east, and Seventh Street on the south. Today the area is home to the Pacific Stock Exchange, Hospital of the Good Samaritan, Belmont High School, and the historic Lewis house. Among other historic highlights, Crown Hill was the site of the first oil discovery in the city by Edward L. Doheny and his partner, Charles A. Canfield, who brought in their first well near the intersection of West Second Street and Glendale Boulevard in 1892. In her first book, Ms. Comer traced the history of Crown Hill from ancient times down to the 1980s, augmenting the text with select historic photographs. Her second book on the Witmers was both a family and pictorial history, centered in the Crown Hill area. These two books established Ms. Comer as a local historian of distinction. Her books are well researched and beautifully written. Her prose is crisp and stylish.

These same characteristics are found in her history of Angels Flight. As in her previous books, Ms. Comer traces the history of Bunker Hill, the site of Angels Flight, with concise and careful detail. She then takes the reader into the beginnings of Angels Flight, detailing the handiwork of Colonel J. Ward Eddy. The history of Angels Flight from its opening in 1901 until its closure in 1969 forms the core of the narrative that follows. Fortunately for those with an historic bent, when the railroad was dismantled it was put into storage. There it was to languish for more than a quarter of a century, rusting, decaying, almost forgotten.

But there is a happy ending. Angels Flight was not *completely* forgotten. It was destined to be rescued by an enlightened group of dedicated individuals who fought the cause for restoration and eventual replacement of the railroad close to its original site. That triumph in the cause of historic preservation is a fitting climax to Ms. Comer's splendid tribute to those involved with Angels Flight, past and present. Here is local history at its best: entertaining, factual, fascinating, informative, and thorough in its presentation, complimented with vintage photographs which supplement the narrative. There is no question: this well-crafted history of Angels Flight is an important contribution to Los Angeles history and a testament to historic conservation.

Doyce B. Nunis, Jr., Ph.D.
Editor, *Southern California Quarterly*

ACKNOWLEDGEMENTS

First and foremost appreciation goes to Dr. Thomas Andrews, Executive Director of the Historical Society of Southern California for his diligent editing and patient guidance of the book through the shoals of publication.

Leigh Ann Hahn and Trisha Harvey have my appreciation for their unstinting administrative support.

For cooperation in securing photographs and documents, acknowledgement is made to the following: Community Redevelopment Agency; Harris & Associates; Pueblo Contracting Services; Tetra Design; The Yellin Company; the History Department of the Los Angeles City Public Library and Tom Owen; Seaver Center for Western History Research; Los Angeles City Archives; Special Collections at California State University, Northridge; History Center at the University of Southern California; Huntington Library; Los Angeles Conservancy; Cultural Affairs Department of the City of Los Angeles; Atlantic-Richfield Archives and Photography Department; Michael Yakaitis of the Library of Moving Images, and Marc Wanamaker of Bison Archives.

Valuable help was received from James Coughlin and Gypsy Cherryholmes, descendants of Colonel James Ward Eddy; from Charles and Kay Richey, relatives of Robert M. Moore, and from Robert, Barbara, Nancy and Greg Moreland, relatives of Helen and Lester Moreland.

Finally, a thank you to everyone who took time to share information about Angels Flight and Bunker Hill.

Virginia L. Comer

CONTENTS

ILLUSTRATIONS

Angels Flight, early 1902, showing open-canopied cars, simple arch without signage or symbolic angel. Courtesy Seaver Center for Western History Research.

Chapter One

Ascent of Angels

In 1901 local newspapers heralded major events from the death of Britain's Queen Victoria in January to the assassination of President William McKinley in September. On a brighter note, an historic moment in the annals of Downtown Los Angeles was being recorded the last day of that year with the opening of an incline railway.

It was 10:00 a.m. on a sunny and mild Tuesday morning December 31, 1901, when an enthusiastic crowd was given the first opportunity to ride the Los Angeles cable cars of Colonel James Ward Eddy's Angels Flight. Running the steep ascent between Downtown's Hill Street and Bunker Hill's Olive Street, Angels Flight served as a connecting link between the shops and businesses on Hill and Broadway and the residences of Bunker Hill.

The Los Angeles *Daily Times* reported, with tongue-in-cheek, Mayor Meredith Pinxton Snyder's "Ascent of the Angels' Flight." Owner-operator Colonel Eddy had passed out handbills announcing that the Mayor would arrive in the first car. Along with City Council members, Eddy had been a passenger on the Flight's premiere public climb. When the car appeared at the Olive Street platform and the Mayor was not on board, "a low moan of disappointment was wrung from the crowd." The fifth ascent was made and still no Mayor. Finally, in the sixth car, the Mayor was seen standing up front. The crowd cheered; the Mayor waved his hat.

After his safe arrival at the Olive Street terminus, the Mayor made a speech in which he referred to the time in his youth when he stood on the top of Bunker Hill looking at "Workman's Empire" in Boyle Heights. Snyder contrasted that view with the metropolis he saw below the Hill in 1901. Colonel Eddy's remarks included reference to the safety of his railway. Their talks highlighted the successful launch of Angels Flight.

Bearing rooftop signage, "L. A. Electric Incline R. R.," the open-canopied cars, traveling under iron pipe arches decorated with electric-light bulbs, made their first public ascent up the eastern slope of Bunker Hill. The Olivet and Sinai, had seating for ten passengers in each of the cars, which were painted an angelic off-white. Specifically, the metal-framed cars with decorative wrought-iron side rails, were an oil base cream color.

For the premiere excursion, riders did not pass under Hill Street's simple arch. Passengers boarded on the south side of the track. A slotted wooden barrier blocked the lower section of the archway with its narrow arch spanning two long, slender columns.

At the Olive Street terminus, on a table decorated with bunting, punch and cookies were served by the ladies of Olive Heights, as that section of Bunker Hill was known. To insure the safety of all riders, the ladies were offering only non-alcoholic punch. Any popping of champagne corks on this New Year's Eve day was deferred to private celebrations.

More than a quarter of a century after Bunker Hill was named, the last best answer to its pedestrian ascent and descent was engineered by a relative newcomer to the City of Angels. Colonel James Ward Eddy arrived in Los Angeles in 1895 and just six years later petitioned the City Council for a permit to run a railway. At the time Eddy came to Los Angeles, Broadway was the center of business and the site of a new City Hall, an elaborate stone structure. In 1901 Eddy was Manager of the Kern-Rand Company and a resident of South Hill Street. No doubt the Los Angeles newcomer, along with his teenaged grandson, took note of the mansions handsomely silhouetted on the hill west of the Colonel's residence. Eddy family records indicate that S. Eddy Gillette first suggested the Flight concept, which his grandfather went on to build. Young Eddy Gillette would continue to invent work-saving devices and have a life-time connection with railroads.

As one acquainted with narrow gauge railways, Colonel Eddy knew the cable incline was a solution for easier access to the eastern slope of Bunker Hill. Eddy was aware of Andrew Hallidie's success with cable cars in San Francisco, however, by the time Colonel Eddy had decided to apply the idea of an electric cable car to the problem of Bunker Hill's steep grade, local cable cars were no longer running. This realization was no deterrent to Eddy's determination to build an incline railway up the slope of Downtown's most prominent hill.

Colonel Eddy's innovative answer to the problem of getting up and down the formidable grade of Bunker Hill was a funicular. From Latin meaning cord or cable, the funicular was celebrated in Luigi Denza's composition, "Funiculi, Funicula," to commemorate the opening of an incline in 1880 on the slopes of Mt. Vesuvius. Visitors could ride to within 450 feet of

Simeon Eddy Gillette in the original station house of his grandfather's incline railway, 1902. Courtesy Eddy family collection.

the crater in the cable railway which was later destroyed by the spectacular eruption in 1944. Widely used in Europe's mountainous regions, the funicular is pulled by a cable. Since the two cars are counter-balanced, a small electric motor is capable of providing sufficient power to overcome friction.

 Eddy's personal stamp was on Angels Flight from the moment he gave his railway a name. Reportedly the cable cars were designated for the Biblical mountains of Olive and Sinai. Angels Flight initially followed the contour of the eastern slope of the promontory with its gradual ascent to Clay Street, named for the deposits of clay used by early local brickmakers. The railway continued up the much steeper climb from Clay to the terminus at Olive Street, where the owner-engineer had built a light metal-framed station house with a pavilion and park. Los Angeles' City Council had passed a resolution naming the ground adjoining the line, Eddy Park. This landscaped park, "adorned with green lawns and spouting fountains," was referred to by the Colonel as Angel's Rest.

At the Olive Street summit, near the crest on public land directly over the Third Street Tunnel, the enterprising Colonel Eddy had constructed a steel observation tower reaching 100 feet. A camera obscura provided a panoramic view of the City of Los Angeles. Meaning "dark chamber," a camera obscura is a box with a double convex lens at the front and a mirror set at a 45 degree angle. An image is transmitted through the lens and appears on the mirror where it is reflected upward on a ground-glass screen at the top of the box. Robert F. Jones, Santa Monica's mayor, who was an aficionado of camera obscuras, had made a gift of the camera which would become a magnet to thousands who would climb Eddy's tower for a spectacular view of the growing city below.

A ride in one of the open-canopied cars that last day of December would have offered a close look at the homes bordering the Flight on the south side. Attractive and well-tended, the two and three-story homes and a three-story apartment building were dwarfed by the Crocker mansion at the top of the hill on Olive Street. Down at the Hill Street entrance, near the southwest corner, a large, mature tree occasionally served as a bulletin board for pertinent notices. Pedestrians and a captive audience of waiting passengers could read the notices, often advertising rooms for rent.

Before the tunnel was completed in 1901, Third Street west from Hill Street had stopped abruptly at Clay. Beyond that the grade of the hillside became much steeper with only a pedestrian walk of steps and ramps. From Olive, Third Street continued westward. A glance up the short section of Third from Hill Street at the turn of the century, revealed a neighborhood of quiet, small-town charm with houses bordered by leafy trees.

Site selection for Angels Flight was most propitious. Third Street, geographically the longest and steepest of the accessible roads, was approximately the center of Bunker Hill. Economically the development of the

Overview of Angels Flight with camera obscura visible on the observation tower, 1907. Courtesy Graphic Arts, CRA.

Mt. Lowe's "Railway in the Clouds" offered a thrilling ride and a smogless vista high above Altadena. 1928 photo courtesy Charles Seims collection.

business district below the Hill and the density of homes on the Hill favored a continual source of riders for the little incline.

Earliest official documentation of Downtown's famous funicular began in the spring of 1901. It was May 10th when Colonel Eddy petitioned City Council for a franchise to operate his electric cable railway. Among the relevant Bunker Hill property owners signing the lawyer-engineer's petition were Judge Julius Brousseau and Mrs. Edward B. Crocker, whose towering mansion bordered the terminus of the Flight. Ten days later Ordinance No. 6576 was granted. When Mayor Meredith Snyder signed the construction authorization on May 25th, there was a stipulation that a free stairway be built on the north side of the funicular to preclude a monopoly on the access to Bunker Hill's steep ascent. The public walkway consisted of 123 steps and ramps, which varied from 3 to 115 feet in length. The second condition to the construction of a railway in the public right of way was the requirement that the area above the Third Street Tunnel be turned into a landscaped park.

That spring the Los Angeles *Herald,* reporting on the proposed construction, referred to Colonel Eddy's elevator lift: "Chariots, which will be manufactured in the City, will be four by ten feet in size and the seats will be elevated as are those of the Mt. Lowe Railway." Spring passed and on the second day of August 1901 construction began and was completed just short of five months.

Though Colonel Eddy would advertise his incline as "the shortest railway in the world," Dubuque, Iowa already had that claim in the Phenelon Place Elevator, built in 1882, with just one ore car. In 1884, the single ore car was replaced with two cable cars carrying eight passengers each. The little railway traveled 296 feet from Downtown Dubuque to a residential area on a bluff overlooking the city and the Mississippi River. Even before the Phenelon Place Elevator made its way uphill in the single ore car, one of the first inclines in the United States, had opened in Pittsburgh on May 28, 1870. Today two Pittsburgh inclines, The Duquesne and The Monongahela, are still in operation. Each railway has a single cable car traveling on parallel tracks.

Southern California had its own history of cable incline railways. Opened on July 4, 1893, Mt. Lowe's Great Incline Railway offered passengers a thrilling ride for approximately 3000 linear feet up grades as steep as 52 per cent. After four decades of scenic passage, the incline ceased its run when a 1936 forest fire destroyed Mt. Lowe's lofty Alpine Tavern. The tracks were ruined later in a flood and the railway was never restored.

On Bunker Hill, in the earliest years of the 1900s, residents were just getting accustomed to riding Angels Flight when a second funicular was constructed a few blocks north on the eastern slope of the hill. Court Flight opened in 1904 at 208 North Broadway between First and Temple. The railway was a 2' 6" parallel two track funicular with a 335 foot elevation up a grade of 46 per cent. Like Angels Flight, there was a stairway access on the north side of the railway, though steeper and longer with 140 steps (47, a landing and 93 to the top). Unlike its neighboring incline, Court Flight was devoid of ornate architectural features on its lower level entrance or its hilltop terminus. Though the fourteen-passenger cars appear to have been a similar light color, they were boxy and lacked any defining features. The Los Angeles *Times* described them as "Quaint and creaky . . . Toonerville cable cars."

Taking a cue from Colonel Eddy's tower attraction, Court Flight had its own observation tower with a large sign announcing, "One Big Look." By the 1930s Big-Look tower had disappeared. A small brick sandwich shop with a striped awning was still doing business at lower level entrance of Court Flight.

Samuel G. Vandegrift of Los Angeles built then operated Court Flight. In the golden age of Bunker Hill's social scene, Court Flight carried tourists, residents and visitors up and down the hill for business and social pursuits in much the same manner as Angels Flight. In 1932 Annie M. Vandegrift took over operation of the railway after the death of her husband.

Each year brought inexorable changes to Bunker Hill resulting in more parking lot spaces for workers at the Civic Center. A photo, circa 1929, taken from the top of Court Flight shows rows of parked cars and a straight-ahead view of the new City Hall on Spring Street. In the 1930s Court Flight carried about 1,000 riders per day, most of them using the parking lots, which charged little or nothing at that time. With the advent of World War II, ridership on Court Flight took a precipitous drop. In August 1942 only one-third of the usual riders were on the Court Street funicular.

A 1920s view of Court Flight at 208 South Broadway with Hotel Broadway on the right. Courtesy Huntington Library.

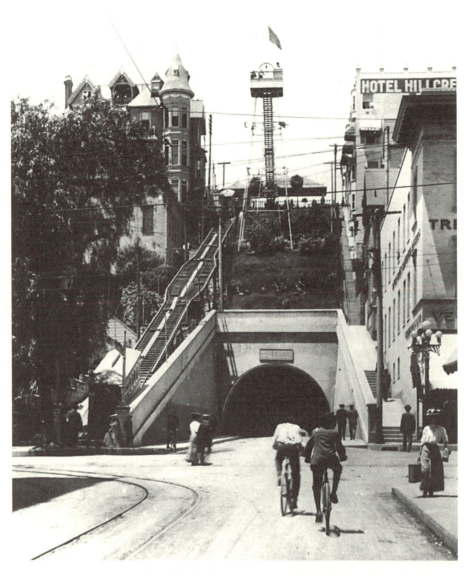

By 1908 business has already begun to encroach on the residential area around Angels Flight. Courtesy Graphic Arts, CRA.

One explanation was the fact that tires and gasoline were rationed, limiting the use of automobiles. Riders were urged to ride the bus or rails. According to the *Times,* owner-operator Mrs. Vandegrift had another complaint: She had no one to run the funicular; her two engineers were doing war-related work. Mrs. Vandegrift petitioned the Board of Public Utilities on September 15, 1942, to discontinue the service. Fifteen days later her petition was granted and operations ceased the following day.

Almost exactly a year later, on September 19, 1943, fire ravaged the site of the abandoned funicular. The blaze was attributed to a cigarette tossed aside, sparking flames in the underbrush and on to the railway ties. There was no substantial evidence of arson. A permit to abandon the facility was issued by the city in 1943 and a year later the ruins of Court Flight were dismantled. Perhaps because it had been used more by commuters parking on the hill than by residents of the area and because it was less of a tourist attraction than its neighbor on Third and Hill, there has been an ebbing of memories of Bunker Hill's other funicular, Court Flight.

With its novel launching that last day of 1901, Angels Flight captivated Los Angeles and never lost its appeal. The incline railway had the advantage of being both utilitarian and recreational and it fulfilled both functions to everyone's satisfaction. Residents on Bunker Hill had easier access to their lofty homes; tourists and city-gazers had the pleasure of railing up for a splendid view of downtown Los Angeles.

The appearance of the elegantly simple funicular with a celestial name enhanced Bunker Hill's grandeur by connecting the neighborhood of the Hill with the business district at its feet. Yet, the planning and execution of the cable railway would have been unnecessary without the presence of Downtown's steep promontory, Bunker Hill. Historically, the two are irrevocably tied.

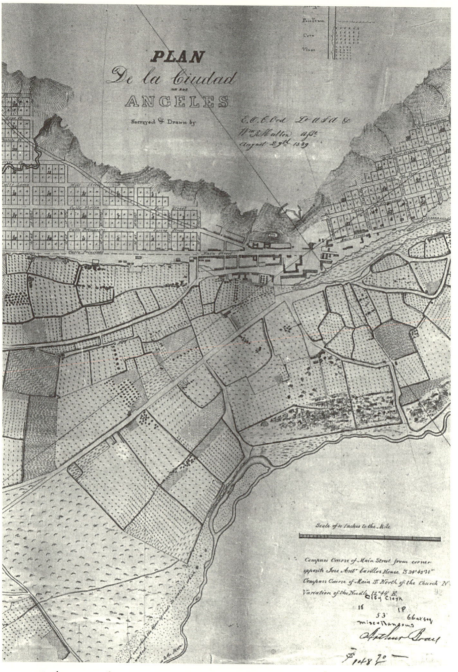

Ord's original survey, August 1849, emphasizing the main residential area of Los Angeles at the fringes of Bunker Hill. Courtesy Seaver Center for Western History Research.

Chapter Two

The Hill From Barren to Bunker

Visiting Southern California on a Yale geological survey, William Brewer camped out on a hill above a picturesque flat-roofed town with vineyards. He wrote in his journal, "the town lies at our feet . . . to the southwest is the Pacific, blue in the distance." Young Brewer pronounced it "a most lovely locality; all that is wanted naturally to make it a paradise is water, more water." Had the geologist stayed around for seasonal changes, he might have seen the picturesque town with the dust of summer at pollution levels or the clay-like mud of winter rains bogging down the local transportation.

With a population of just under five thousand, the town at Brewer's feet was Los Angeles in 1860; the hill may have been Bunker. It was the dominant hill west of the area where the forty-four pobladores had settled in September 1781 to form the nucleus of the pueblo which became Los Angeles. Sixty-eight years later, in June 1849, Military Governor Bennett Riley of the territorial government in Monterey ordered a city map to be made, "to serve as a basis for granting vacant lots out of unappropriated lands belonging to the Municipality."

Financially drained by the recent war with Mexico, Los Angeles was in need of money. This municipal land sale would set the stage for the City's first subdivision and would continue unabated until only the park lands of Pershing, Elysian and the Plaza were left of the pueblo's original four square leagues. According to one historian, "Even the site of the present City Hall had to be bought back."

West Point Lt. Edward Otho Cresap Ord, stationed at Monterey, had been recommended by Military Governor Riley. After two weeks of negotiation, Ord was chosen to be the surveyor whose task was the preparation of a city map. Since Army wages were meager, officers often accepted outside employment. Initially Lt. Ord, who had arrived in Los Angeles on July 3, offered to survey the town for $3,000, but on July 18 he asked for "compensation of fifteen hundred dollars in coin, ten lots selected from among those demarked in the map and vacant land to the extent of one thousand varas." (A vara is a Latin American unit of linear measure which varies in different countries from 32 to 43 inches. A square vara is also referred to simply as a vara.) Ord specified that if the

Like a beached whale, a nearly barren Bunker Hill is a dark land mass to the right of

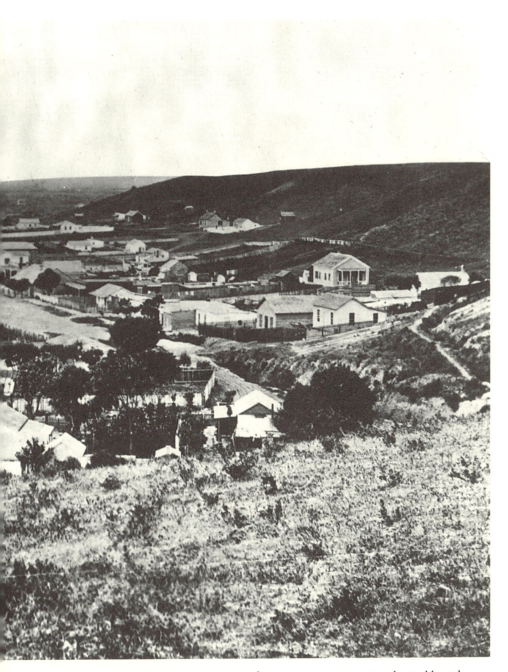

old Fort Street (Broadway) in an 1864 photo. Courtesy Los Angeles Public Library.

coin and land offer as payment was denied, he would accept the sum
of $3,000 in cash. The City Council decided it was in their interest to
keep the land and give Ord the money.

Ord's survey covered the heart of the pueblo, extending from the
river to the hills and nearly to Campo Santo (the cemetery). Mapping
did not extend up into the hills. From late July to September 19, 1849,
when the map was turned over to the City Council, Ord worked with his
assistant William Rich Hutton, who sketched historic scenes of the pueblo
environs in his spare moments. As a result of Ord's survey, fifty-four lots
were sold at the city's first auction on November 7th and by the end of
December the city had realized nearly $2,500, almost recovering the cost
of Ord's survey. Lots in the more favored area, bounded by Second and
Fourth, Spring and Hill streets, commanded as much as $200 while
lots in the older part of town, north of the Plaza, fared less well, going
for as little as $50.

While Ord quietly mapped the streets of Los Angeles, gold
seekers rushed to San Francisco, bypassing the pueblo of Los Angeles,
of which John W. Audubon wrote in his 1849 journal, "An antiquated,
dilapidated air prevades all." In the late 1850s the fledgling city's business
district functioned in what is now the area of Downtown's civic center
at Main, Spring and Temple streets while a few blocks west the steep
hill loomed nearly barren.

In a brief period of high wool prices the dry promontory, 136
acres of treeless chaparral with sagebrush, cactus, wild mustard and winter
grass, was used to graze sheep; at other times cattle occasionally fed on the
hillside. Years would pass before the unnamed and prominent hill with the
town at its feet would become a residential enclave. Seemingly unapproach-
able, the heights did appeal to those citizens with a tendency to seek higher
elevations, especially with the flooding of lower areas in the rainy season.

In 1852 Prudent Beaudry, a French Canadian, came to town. An
energetic, enterprising man who would later become mayor of Los Angeles,
he would be listed as one of the wealthiest men in Los Angeles County just
eight years after his arrival. Lured to California in the gold rush, Beaudry
had been in the mercantile business in San Francisco; in Los Angeles he
was buying land. Following the flood of 1861, a drought in 1862 and the
smallpox epidemic in 1863, Beaudry bought 20 acres of the city's imposing

land mass at a sheriff's auction in 1867 for $517. Beaudry's steep hillside plot was bordered by Second, Fourth, Hill and Charity (Grand) Streets. There was some immediate value in the clay pits found on the property.

Aware of the other possibilities on the substantial hill, Prudent Beaudry attempted to acquire the rest of the acreage by public auction and in that regard submitted a map, rendered by surveyor George Hansen, indicating the desired area: Street of the Grasshoppers (Figueroa) to Hill Street, bounded by Temple Street on the north and Beaudry's 20 acres on the south. Stephen H. Mott, however, had the same idea. Mott, who would later become secretary of the Los Angeles City Water Company, was a deputy in the office of his brother, Thomas D. Mott, City Clerk. Stephen Mott ordered a survey of the available property and ended up with rest of the acreage on Bunker Hill.

Surveyor George Hansen kept trade diaries, a collection of small leather journals from 1866-1890 which contain entries of his mappings and surveys. His notes indicate that he made several maps in 1867 and 1868 for Beaudry, who continued to extend his real estate holdings south of Bunker Hill. The local paper, the Los Angeles *Star,* had remarked on Beaudry's earlier 20-acre subdivision, predicting that the lots on Bunker Hill would double in value in one year.

By the spring of 1869 Beaudry's lots were successfully auctioned with the developer clearing $30,000 on Grand and Hill Street properties. In a period of surging growth for the residential area, Beaudry had also subdivided nearly 40 acres south and west of his initial 20 acre investment on Bunker Hill. Located between Fourth and Grand, Sixth and Figueroa, the properties netted Beaudry an additional $50,000.

Beaudry had offered his lands on the installment plan: $15 down and $15 a month for lots priced $100 to $525. However, there was yet another hurdle for Beaudry. It was not merely the steepness of the hill's ascent which had prevented settlement, it was more specifically a lack of water. Los Angeles' early subdivider solved that dilemma in 1868 when, along with two associates, he formed the Los Angeles City Water Company. By late 1872 Beaudry had installed 11 miles of iron pipe over the highest hills in the area. A steam-driven Hooker pump with a 40,000 gallon-an-hour capacity filled two small reservoirs built at an elevation of 240 feet. Water was pumped from the old Abila springs to Beaudry's hillside

Downtown Los Angeles late 1880s. Church, upper right, is on the SE corner of Second and Broadway and looks due east to St. Vibiana's Cathedral. Courtesy Seaver Center for Western History Research.

property. As a founding officer of the Los Angeles City Water Company, Beaudry set the same rates for hill dwellers as for patrons in the city below. A sampling of the fees shows that there was a charge of $2 for a family of not more than five persons living in a tenement. For private homes there was a fee of twenty-five cents per tub while owners of private water closets were charged $1 per W.C. Even the washing of horses had a price, $1 per ownership of horse and carriage.

Ten years after its formation in 1868, the private Los Angeles City Water Company hired a young Irish immigrant as a zanjero (ditch tender). Early in 1902 the city, finally acquiring rights to water distribution, established the Los Angeles Water Works, which was quickly renamed the Water Department. That year former zanjero William Mulholland became the first superintendent of what would be known as the Department of Water and Power.

While Bunker Hill's water problem had been solved, there remained the issue of accessibility. James Wesley Potts, a purchaser of Hill lots, spent more than $30,000 in the four years between 1872 and 1876 grading Temple and Second Streets to make those lots more accessible. Pedestrians in 1887 had the option of using a public stairway which zigzagged from upper to lower Third Street.

The rapid increase of homes on Bunker Hill was augmented by more efficient methods of building. The "balloon frame" technique using nailed 2 x 4s meant that construction of homes no longer required heavy timbers. With less expensive Douglas Fir available, cottages could be purchased for only $2,000 or a two-story home for $5,000. All that and an incomparable view.

Meanwhile Los Angeles was in the throes of an historic land boom, described by Harris Newmark in his reminiscences as a "violent boom" with "symptoms of feverish excitement." Newmark noted that in the summer of 1887 the well advertised charms of climate and scenery, combined with the efforts of the Chamber of Commerce and Board of Trade, had been successful to the extent that thousands of Easterners swelled the number already in Los Angeles. Extension of the Southern Pacific eastward and construction of the Santa Fe Railroad brought tourists who stayed through the summer and then looked for permanent homesteads. Adding to the area's paradisial appeal were the scent and accessible fruit of millions of bearing orange trees. By spring of 1888 the land boom was over.

In the interim Prudent Beaudry continued to improve conditions on Bunker Hill. Generously he donated miles of streets and spent $200,000 to have them opened and graded. Beaudry's generosity appeared not to be motivated by overt self-aggrandizement. No street on Bunker Hill bore his name. In 1883, just ten years before his death at the age of 75, Beaudry Avenue was named in his honor. Located just west of Figueroa, Beaudry Avenue runs through Crown Hill.

The year hill developer Prudent Beaudry was elected Mayor of Los Angeles, 1875, Downtown's steep promontory received a formal designation. On the 100th anniversary of a famous and decisive battle of the Revolutionary War, Downtown Los Angeles' most prominent land mass was given the name of that battle, Bunker Hill.

Bradbury Mansion circa 1888. Sketch by Ilma Cunningham.

Chapter Three

Mansions on the Hill

The first recorded structure on Bunker Hill was not a Victorian mansion, not a residence at all but a small church. Former slave Biddy Mason had organized the First African Methodist Episcopal Church in 1872 in her home at 331 South Spring Street. Later the enterprising nurse-midwife bought a lot on Bunker Hill and the African Methodist Episcopal Church was built on what would become the intersection of Charity (Grand Avenue) and Fourth Street, described at the time as a grassy bluff.

Just west of their hillside homes, Bunker Hill's youth could swim in a pond formed by a creek running from the Echo Park Reservoir, known as a zanja (ditch). Underground springs in a canyon near Downtown had been tapped as a source of water for the city after a dam was constructed across that canyon by the Canal and Reservoir Company. George Hansen, surveyor of land on Bunker Hill, was president of the Canal and Reservoir Company.

The recollections of Sarah Bixby Smith offer a look inside a Bunker Hill residence in the early 1880s and a description of the area of the first Bixby home near Grand Avenue. "Temple Street was new and open for only a few blocks. Bunker Hill Avenue was the end of the settlement . . . along the ridge fringing the sky. Beyond that we looked over empty, grassy hills to the mountains." A few years later Sarah's father had a family home built on the south-east corner of Court and Hill streets, a seven-room cottage, which would have a second story added later. Even with the addition of a second story, the Bixby residence would be dwarfed when the Bradbury mansion was built on an opposite corner of Court and Hill.

What the Bixby house did have was a large sitting room whose "colors were kept in harmony with a key color, a medium olive relieved by soft shades of rose and tan." According to Smith, the room was furnished with four bookcases, a rosewood square piano, a large walnut table, a sofa and several easy chairs, family portraits, original paintings as well as reproductions of the masters. At the end of the room a white marble mantel formed a distinct line above the grate on which coal burned.

With the availability of water, mansions blossomed on the Hill, displaying architecture of Gothic and Victorian splendor; homes with

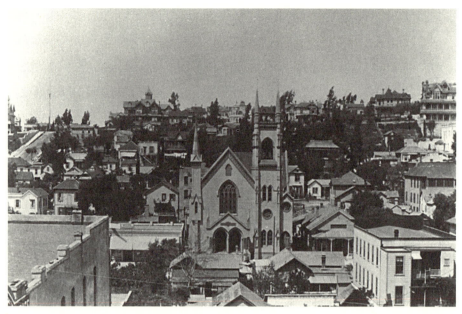

Bunker Hill, 1880s, with Crocker Mansion on the right, Fourth Street on the left. Church is 337 S. Broadway, current site of Grand Central Market. Author's collection.

turrets, towers, cupolas, dormers, gables, balconies, bay windows circular and square, leaded and stained glass windows, tall brick chimneys, fluted columns, fish-scale shingles and wrap-around porches ornamented with spools and spindles. Bunker Hill had become an elegant neighborhood, home to some of Los Angeles' most historic and prominent families.

By 1876 the Queen Anne design had became a popular choice of prospective homeowners and this style was exemplified by the work of the Newsom brothers, Samuel and Joseph Cather. One of their architectural jewels was the Bunker Hill Bradbury mansion, considered by J. C. Newsom as the finest residence in Los Angeles. Located at 406 Court on the corner of Hill and Court, the mansion reigned as a model of elegant Victorian detail. A splendid Queen Anne design, emphatic with towers and turrets, the exterior displayed ornamentation of a cactus pattern which, as a native plant, architect Newsom felt it was proper to use. Built in 1887 the three-story structure cost $80,000.

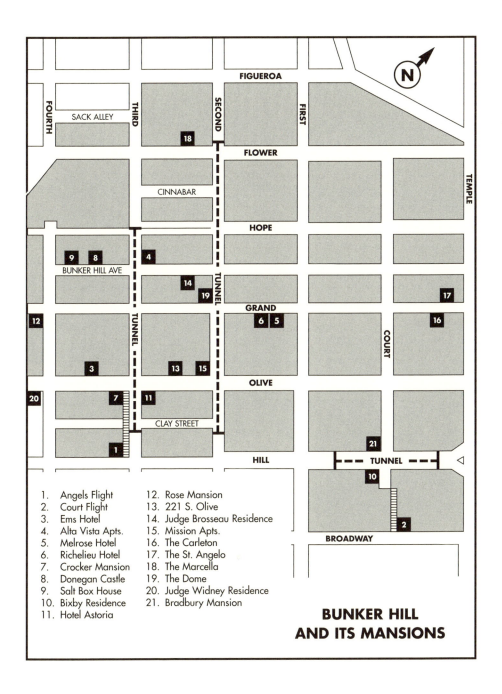

BUNKER HILL
AND ITS MANSIONS

1. Angels Flight
2. Court Flight
3. Ems Hotel
4. Alta Vista Apts.
5. Melrose Hotel
6. Richelieu Hotel
7. Crocker Mansion
8. Donegan Castle
9. Salt Box House
10. Bixby Residence
11. Hotel Astoria
12. Rose Mansion
13. 221 S. Olive
14. Judge Brosseau Residence
15. Mission Apts.
16. The Carleton
17. The St. Angelo
18. The Marcella
19. The Dome
20. Judge Widney Residence
21. Bradbury Mansion

J. C. Newsom described the thirty-room residence as having large salon parlors, decorated ceilings and hardwood floors throughout the house. "The library is to the right as you enter; the bookcases are built around this room to a height of 8 feet. The room is finished in wood, 'no plaster'. The dining room is finished in oak 'quartered antique' and has paneled ceilings and sidewalls. There is a large, fine domed ceiling in the billiard room with a card room attached. The exterior of the residence is granite, marble, wood and shingles." This succinct summary of the large and magnificent mansion was part of the architect's advertisement and did not begin to elaborate on the detailing of fine woods, the windows and miscellaneous embellishments.

Lewis Leonard Bradbury and his wife Simona Martinez had entertained the elite of Los Angeles society in their showplace residence. Their son John would marry the lovely socialite Lucy Tichnor Banning, daughter of transportation pioneer Phineas Banning, joining two prominent local families. John and Lucy Bradbury made their home, a relatively modest two-story design, at 247 North Bunker Hill Avenue. Unfortunately, neither the marriage nor the distinctive paternal mansion had a happy ending. A permit to raze the inimitable residence, with an estimated demolition cost of $850, was issued January 16, 1929. The marriage, lasting only nine years, had an even shorter life.

Money from a Mexican silver mine had paved the way for the sumptuous residence of Bradbury, who also built one of Los Angeles' most distinctive office buildings. A brick and terra cotta structure designed by George Herbert Wyman, the Bradbury Building graces the corner of Third and Broadway. A National Historic Landmark, the Bradbury presents a central court whose balcony and stair railings are wrought iron decorated in an arabesque design; handrails are polished mahogany and the stairways Italian marble. Ornamented with the same French ironwork, a pair of cage elevators offers spectators a look at the workings of the handsome cast iron mechanism as the elevators rise with slow grace. Light from the five-story height of the skylight floods the central court.

A few months before the completion of what architectural doyenne Esther McCoy referred to as, "A Vast Hall of Light," Lewis L. Bradbury died. Though he never lived to enjoy his $500,000 monument,

Bradbury Building, incomparable opus of architect George Herbert Wyman.
Photo Downtown Exposure, author's collection.

*Looking north on Grand Avenue in 1900. Upper right, stone courthouse at
Spring and Temple. Courtesy Seaver Center for Western History Research.*

Bradbury's name and the ageless beauty of his building have a
permanent place in the history of Los Angeles.

At 325 South Bunker Hill Avenue a three-story mansion of
twenty rooms combined a classic style with the ostentation of the Victorian
period, exemplified by ornate scrollwork. Characterizing the best of this
late nineteenth century craftsmanship was a fine hardwood stairway with
four-feet high hand-carved newel posts, which were once topped with
ornamental gas lamps. Front doors with leaded art glass were set back
under a broadly arched and finely detailed front entrance. Built in 1882
the mansion was notable for its gingerbread porte-cochere and distinctive,
elongated carriage house. Later the mansion was sold to Daniel Francis
Donegan. An engineer, Donegan ran a contracting company which built

the first railroad from Los Angeles to Pasadena. The Donegan mansion came to be known as "The Castle" with a reputation for mystery. Chapter Eight reveals the cruel twist fate had waiting for the early Bunker Hill showplace.

Bunker Hill resident Judge Robert McClay Widney, a tall, attractive man with chin whiskers, qualified as a civil and hydraulic engineer, a botanist, a title expert in Mexican and Spanish land grants, a mathematician, geologist, mineralogist and a dead shot with a pistol. From the time he arrived in Los Angeles in 1868 with his wife, Mary Barnes, a former College of the Pacific classmate, Widney began making his historical mark on the City. Combining the practice of law with the sale of real estate, Widney published a monthly paper, the Los Angeles *Real Estate Advertiser.*

In 1873 when the Widney family lived on Hill Street, at the current site of the Subway Terminal Building, Judge Widney had his office in the Plaza area. Since he enjoyed going home for the lunch recess, Widney decided to establish a horsecar line. A franchise was secured for a line to run from the Pico House on Main Street, to Spring and First Street, on to Fort (Broadway) out to Fourth and Hill, down Sixth Street and over to Pearl (Figueroa) where stables and car shed were located. Neighbors were asked to cooperate and assess themselves fifty cents per front foot of property. A year later (1874) the two and one-half mile "Sixth and Spring" Line was in operation, charging passengers ten cents a ride, or for twenty-five cents a patron could buy five slugs, good for one ride each.

In 1880 Widney, with his neighbor Edward F. Spence, his brother Dr. Joseph Widney and three others, founded the University of Southern California. By 1895 the Widneys had moved to 416 South Olive. The charming Bunker Hill residence would be the scene of the wedding of the Widneys' daughter Frances to Boyle Workman, son of two pioneer families.

State Senator Leonard John Rose was the master of a palatial 6,000 foot residence, created by Curlett and Eissen. Located on the southeast corner of Fourth and Grand, the home was considered a splendid example of "American Renaissance" style. Rose, whose sister was the wife of attorney Stuart O'Melveny, had been a successful fruit-

Front view of Crocker Mansion at 300 S. Olive, 1880s.
Courtesy Seaver Center For Western History Research.

grower, vintner and racehorse breeder. His Rosemeade Stock Farms, home of highly bred champion trotting horses, bore the name of the present City of Rosemead. Senator Rose had developed a variety of foreign grapes which were prized in the wine industry. When he sold the Sunny Slope Estate, 2,000 acres of orchards and vineyards, he received over a million dollars. L. J. Rose was fifty years old in 1887 when he moved to Los Angeles where he had purchased a 100' x 100' lot on Bunker Hill. A massive retaining wall of granite was built around the lot, which was one of the highest points in the residential district.

A reporter for the Los Angeles *Evening Express*, in October of 1890, doing a column on beautiful homes of Los Angeles, was enthralled with the elegance of the Rose mansion and its ornate delights. Description began at the broad front steps of polished granite which led to a tiled veranda and into the entrance hall of antique oak with heavily paneled ceiling. The Express reporter had gone up the staircase where "at the second landing of this oaken work of art there glows an oriel window of jeweled glass, the center panel of which is filled by an amber horn of plenty from which there falls a fluttering shower of wild roses." It was noted that the library walls were a distinctive Pompeian red; the ceiling had been elegantly frescoed by an Italian artist. All the hardware in the house was solid silver. On the top floor there was a dance hall with a tower window which afforded a panoramic view of the city. Not surprisingly, the basement contained an excellent wine cellar.

When the hilltop mansion was finished, the owner presented it to his wife, Amanda, as a gift. The total outlay for this extravagant gift with such exquisite attention to detail was $110,000. Unfortunately, within a decade, Rose's financial fortunes were severely reversed and in 1899, he died by his own hand. A note to his wife explained that he could no longer endure the endless debt. In 1937, Rose's grand old home was leveled reportedly to make space for a gas station.

At the southeast corner of Olive and Third the striking Crocker mansion was a most visible landmark. Immediately adjacent to the station house terminus of Angels Flight, the imposing mansion is readily recognized in early photos of the incline railway. Above a retaining wall, distinctive in its height and mass, two long verandas with elaborate Victorian hand-tooled designs on the supporting columns, were topped by a third level deck. From the less familiar west-facing view of the front

Melrose Hotel (left), Richelieu Hotel (right), S.Grand Avenue,Bunker Hill, 1927.
Courtesy Graphic Arts, CRA.

entrance at 300 South Olive, the Crocker residence appears to be a long-windowed, second-story home with a substantial attic. However, the east-facing view shows the third level built into the hillside above the notable wall.

In 1887 the main occupant of the spacious home was the widow of Edward B. Crocker. Just three years later the City Directory listed the home at 300 South Olive as "Mansion Rooms." In 1899 it was called a family hotel and in 1904 it was billed as furnished rooms. By late 1908 the impressive Victorian had been torn down and on September 2nd of that year a cornerstone was laid with proper pomp and ceremony by the Benevolent and Protective Order of Elks, Los

Angeles Lodge No. 99. On May 6, 1909, at 7:30 p.m. the Elks'
new temple was formally dedicated.

Among other notables on the Hill was Ohio-born Judge
Anson Brunson, a founding member of the Los Angeles Bar Association.
Before attaining his position on the bench, Brunson had been a law
partner of Stuart O'Melveny whose firm, now located on reshaped Bunker
Hill, continues its practice as O'Melveny and Myers. Brunson, considered
a brilliant and witty attorney, had his sumptuous office suite in the brand-
new $450,000 Baker Block, which opened in December of 1878. The
handsome Main Street structure was referred to as the "mecca of every
ambitious L. A. attorney." Brunson lived in a sprawling three-story
residence on Grand north of Fourth Street in a home notable for its
long drawing room.

On the east side of Bunker Hill Avenue, number 238 was
the residence of Judge Julius Brousseau. An accomplished attorney from
Malone, New York, Brosseau, with his wife and four children, came to
Southern California in January of 1877 for reasons of health. Of French
heritage, Brosseau helped to establish the local French Hospital. A charter
member of the Los Angeles Bar Association, Judge Brousseau had a
special interest in water litigation. Brousseau's spacious two-story home
with a tower was often the scene of dinners and parties. Later, like most
Bunker Hill mansions, the Judge's former residence became a low-rental
rooming house.

Located at 350 South Grand, the turreted, three-story stucco
home of philanthropist Myra Hershey presented a variance from the
neighboring wood-framed Victorian mansion of Senator Leonard J.
Rose and most of the other houses on the Hill.

Along with elegant housing in the Victorian era on Bunker
Hill, fine hotels made an appearance. The Los Angeles *Tribune* on July 8,
1887, carried an article stating that since Los Angeles was destined to be
a resort for Eastern businessmen and pleasure-seekers, for the sake of private interests and the advantage of the city, there must be suitable accommodations. By the fall of that year The Melrose, an elegant hotel was
built at 130 South Grand Avenue, between Second and Third streets, on
property owned by Robert Larkin, a prominent Chicago businessman. The
fifty-room establishment, known as a fashionable family hotel, charged

$1.50 to $2 a day for rooms with "all possible conveniences." A three-storied hostelry, The Melrose, distinctive with sizeable towers and gables, was lavish with intricate hand-crafted ornamentation and richly embellished with fish-scale shingles. In the 1950s, photographer Arnold Hylen was impressed with the grace and beauty of the ornate hotel, calling the grand old structure, "surely the queen of the hostelries." Host to visiting socialites of the Victorian day, it was torn down in the late 1950s.

Sharing in Hylen's enthusiastic praise was the handsome Victorian next door to The Melrose. In 1891 the Los Angeles City Directory listed 142 South Grand as the residence of Robert Larkin; later it was known as the Richelieu Hotel. Guests were charged $2 a day to stay at the eighteen-room structure, distinguished by an ornate second-story window which was enclosed and decorated with a carving consisting of a large monogram and a bird. Sitting on top of the intertwined initials, "RL," the bird looked down quizzically. Hylen believed that the Melrose, combined with the neighboring three-story Richelieu Hotel, was "a vivid memento of what the Hill was like in its prime." The Richelieu maintained an outward appearance of grace and elegance until the day it was demolished in the late 1950s. Not all Bunker Hill domiciles were fashioned in such grand Victorian splendor. More modest one and two-story frame houses of the early 1870s had been part of the building boom as well.

Water brought by developer Beaudry had changed Bunker's hillscape from semi-desert to semi-tropical which, during its peak years, helped to graphically define an affluent residential community. Landscaping, which included trees as diverse as palm and jacaranda, shrubs, vines, green lawns, and gardens of floral delights, from the simplicity of colorful nasturtiums to all manner of roses, enhanced the aesthetics of the Hill's architecture.

Coinciding with the land boom and nearly a decade after the debut of the Sixth and Spring Street horse-car line in 1874, Los Angeles would have its first cable car system which would go up and over Bunker Hill on Second and First streets. Banker-businessman Henry Clayton Witmer and associates hired successful engineer Andrew Hallidie of San Francisco's Cable Car fame to construct a similar cable line from Second and Spring Street to its western terminus on Crown Hill's Texas Street

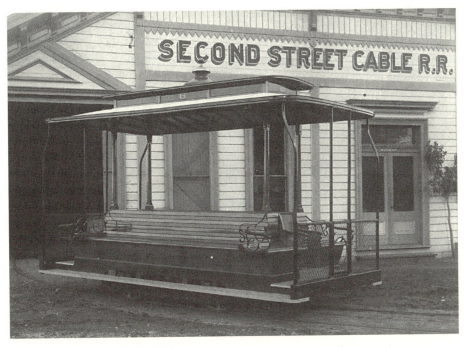

Second Street Cable Car terminus on Crown Hill in 1886.
Courtesy Witmer family collection.

(Belmont Avenue) The Witmer-backed Second Street Cable line climbed grades of more than 25 per cent (one foot up for every four feet).

Though the Second Street Cable Railway was a financial success, it was sold in January 1887. The cable line had served its main purpose, which was to gain access to Witmer-owned lots for sale on Crown Hill, directly west of Downtown. James McLaughlin, the new owner of the Second Street Railway, however, was dogged by misfortune during his two years of running the cable line. When a torrential rain in late December 1889 swept away a long segment of track, it was the end of the line for the city's first cable railway. A decade would pass before the barrier to Bunker Hill's accessibility would be removed.

ANGEL'S FLIGHT

Compliments of J. W. EDDY

Chapter Four

Colonel Eddy and His Celestial Railway

olonel James Ward Eddy came to
Los Angeles as an engineer, but
he had studied for and practiced
law. Born May 30, 1832, in Java,
Wyoming County, New York, less than
50 miles south of Rochester, Eddy
attended the Arcade public schools and
graduated from the Wesleyan Seminary
and Genessee College in Lima, New
York. After teaching school in New York
State, he moved to Illinois in 1853 to
study law. Two years later he was admitted to the bar in Chicago. Moving to
Batavia, about 35 miles from Chicago,
James Ward Eddy, Esquire, married
Isabella Worsley. A man of many interests and activities, he practiced law in
Batavia and became the superintendent
of the local school board. Domestically
he was the father of a daughter Carrie and a son George.

HAVE YOU VISITED *the*

"ANGEL'S FLIGHT?"

If not, why not?

IT IS THE MOST UNIQUE, INTER-
ESTING AND USEFUL IN-
CLINED RAILWAY IN
THE WORLD.

IT is in the heart of the city
—Hill and Third Streets,
Los Angeles, Cal. The ride
is inspiring and perfectly
safe. The view from the
Tower — "Angel's View" — is
grand, overlooking city and
mountains. The camera ob-
scura puts a beautiful living
picture of Third Street and
vicinity on canvas before you.

Fare 5 cents, three for 10 cents,
ten for 25 cents, 100 for $1.00.
Angel's View with Camera Obscura, 5 cents; three for 10
cents. Rest Pavilion, "Angel's
Rest," overlooking city, Eddy
Park and Fountain FREE. Easy
Chairs. Come and bring your
friends and enjoy yourselves.

PHONES: Home 2013, Main 1314

In Illinois Eddy campaigned actively for Abraham Lincoln,
whom he characterized as a friend. When the Civil War broke out,
Eddy promptly enlisted in a battalion recruited to protect the nation's
capitol. With the rank of colonel at the end of the Civil War, Eddy was
elected to the state legislature in Kane County, Illinois in 1866 and
after four years he served in that state's senate. Nearly ten years later
Eddy's career had changed from the field of law to engineering. As
vice-president of the Chicago, Millington & Western Railway, the
Honorable J. W. Eddy made a lengthy appeal to the Chicago Board
of Trade for the railway's admission to the city. In his address Colonel
Eddy emphasized the financial advantage of his company's narrow-
gauge rail with each car carrying 8 tons of weight. Eddy and the
Chicago, Millington & Western Railway received the Board of
Trade's endorsement.

1880s photo of a younger Colonel James Ward Eddy. Courtesy Eddy family collection.

Later Eddy followed the westward expansion as far as Arizona where he was a prospector. In 1881, according to Letters Received, Office of Indian Affairs, Eddy had been one of the first to locate the Deer Creek (San Carlos) coal fields. That same year Eddy conceived the idea of linking the booming town of Globe with the Atlantic and Pacific Railroad. Located 180 miles north of the mining town, the line was a subsidiary of the Santa Fe Railroad. In the two years spent obtaining financial backing, the enterprising Colonel established an office in Boston, home base of the A & P.

In 1883 Eddy was named president of the $8 million dollar Arizona Mineral Belt Railroad. Four years later, in 1887, financial problems brought construction to a halt. With 35 miles still to be completed, the railroad line was terminated at a sheriff's sale in December 1888. Eddy moved to California where he surveyed the proposed transmission line which would bring power from Kern County to Los Angeles. The plant line was later completed in 1904 and is now part of the vast network of the Southern California Edison Company.

Colonel Eddy was 63 when he and his wife Isabella moved to Los Angeles in March 1895. Personal tragedy had made its imprint on the life of James Ward Eddy. Earlier his son George, a civil engineer, had died of consumption at the age of 23 after completing an engineering project for the Aurora, Illinois Electric System. Eddy's wife Isabella was not destined to see her husband's charming and functional railway conquering the eastern slope of Bunker Hill. Shortly after her arrival in the City of Angels, Isabella Eddy died. Later, Colonel Eddy had the remains of his young son sent from Illinois to be interred in the Hollywood Cemetery family plot.

*In 1905 the cars were enclosed; windows were vented or louvered; signage
and a symbolic angel appear on the archway. Courtesy Seaver Center
for Western History Research.*

In the nearly dozen years of his ownership of Angels Flight, Eddy
maintained an involvement in all phases of the railway. It was not long
after the official opening that the physical structure of Angels Flight was
changed. To insure a uniform 33 percent grade from Hill to Olive, the
railway was rebuilt on a wooden trestle in 1905. Clay Street was no longer
intersected by the railway whose cars now passed overhead. At this time the
cable cars underwent a major renovation as well. Despite the charm of the
small open cars with their fine wrought-iron side rails, there were enough
days with chilling wind or inclement weather to warrant their enclosure.
Competition may have been another motive for change. Court Flight's
opening the year before had given Bunker Hill an alternative funicular
whose cars were enclosed and accommodated more passengers.

Instead of the original 10 riders, the new Angels Flight cars, larger and of wood construction, offered seven interior seats on each side and two exterior seats, accommodating a total of 16 passengers. When the run was crowded, two passengers could share a seat for a total of 32 seated riders. With standees there could be a "crush load" of 54 riders per car. Windows, which for safety's sake did not open, were angled and seats were stepped to remain level and accommodate the grade of the slope throughout the ride. Passengers, their backs to the slanted windows, sat facing each other across the narrow aisle.

In the spring of 1910, just five years after the Flight's first renovation, Colonel Eddy embarked on the renovation project which would become a definitive symbol of Angels Flight. In 1910 at the top of Olive Street, Colonel Eddy's original, lightweight metal station house with pavilion was removed and replaced by a new Beaux Arts Classical Revival structure. This first renovation of the station house was eye-catching with six bays visible from the west elevation and five from the east elevation. The white concrete of the distinctive open colonnades and arches with ornate cornice enhanced the dramatic presentation of the new structure on Third and Olive streets. At the Flight's Hill Street entrance, the relatively simple arch, bearing a two-foot angel figure in a flowing robe, was replaced with the Beaux Arts Classical Revival design archway, which remained basically unchanged until it was dismantled in 1969.

During the decade that Colonel Eddy operated his own railway line, he took an active part in its promotion, personally designing an Angels Flight brochure. A feature photo in the pamphlet shows the new, enclosed cable cars which no longer rolled past prestigious residences on flights up and down Bunker Hill; rows of hotels and other commercial buildings had replaced some of the large, pleasant homes. When Eddy's brochure came out, it presented a Third and Hill Street view of the funicular with its ornate arch and the high steel observation tower. Decorated with a small portrait of the founder-builder, the brochure asked, "Have you visited the *Angel's Flight*? If not, why not? It is the most unique, interesting and useful inclined railway in the world." The pamphlet described the ride as "inspiring and perfectly safe." It suggested that visitors bring their friends and enjoy the easy chairs and fountain at Eddy Park "Free."

Station House, 1912, showing the 5 east-facing arches in Train and Williams original Beaux Arts design of 1910. Courtesy Seaver Center for Western History Research.

In a promotional stunt, a Carter Car climbs Angels Flight, 1909.
Courtesy Urban Archives, CSUN, L.A. Public Library.

The success of the Bunker Hill funicular may have been the inspiration for establishing the Mt. Hollywood Scenic Railway Company. In the summer of 1905 the Los Angeles *Daily Journal* reported plans for the intended incline and listed Colonel James Ward Eddy among the backers. In January 1909 the *Journal* ran another item about intentions for a Mt. Hollywood Railway, which never came to fruition.

Not all Hill residents were content to ride Angels Flight and gaze at the city from the vaunted height of the terminus. In May 1904 Mr. W. S. Collins and six associates met to discuss a proposal for two mammoth elevators to take passengers quickly and more cheaply up the Hill. Their idea was to sink a shaft, on private property at the corner of Third and Olive streets, which would connect with the tunnel close to Hill Street. Though the men were quite serious, nothing came of the proposal and there was no real challenge to Colonel Eddy's incline railway.

Boyle Workman, whose name represents pioneer families maternal and paternal, was 33 years old when Eddy's incline railway made its debut. In Workman's account of Los Angeles, *The City That Grew*, he described Colonel Eddy as being widely recognized with his funicular. "Wherever the Colonel went, with his trim whiskers and mustache, his high collars, his military air, he was pointed out as the builder of the famous little railroad which held the record of carrying more passengers per mile than any railroad in the world."

According to railway historian Donald Duke, when Colonel Eddy encountered financial problems with the operation of Angels Flight, he printed an appeal and offered it with each ticket. The notice began: "A Neighborly Word With Patrons of Angels Flight." The verbose but heart-felt appeal worked briefly, then finally Eddy was given permission to increase the price from one-cent to five cents for the round-trip fare.

The relevance of the letters B.P.O.E., just below "Angels Flight" on the entrance archway, pertains to the Benevolent and Protective Order of Elks, Los Angeles Lodge No. 99. In 1909 the fraternal society became the next-door neighbor of Angels Flight at 300 South Olive. When the Elks' Grand Lodge Reunion was held in Los Angeles from July 11 to July 17 that same year, over 60,000 passengers set an all-time record for Colonel Eddy's incline railway. In addition to enjoying Angels Flight, delegates of the reunion had parades with floats and decorated Talleyhos (horse-drawn coaches) to rival those of the early Rose Parades.

At the time of the Elks' Reunion, Angels Flight still had the simple archway and a metal-sided station house. Though visiting Elks were long gone when the new Train & Williams designed structures were completed in 1910, it was reported that the neighboring Elks donated money for the Flight's ornate arch. Their generosity was repaid publicly with the letters B. P. O. E. sculpted at nearly the same size and just below the lettering "Angels Flight."

By 1929 the Elks had moved from the building on Olive, and around that time the B. P. O. E. letters were painted black. Years before the dismantling in May of 1969, the incision of the initials had been filled in, nearly obliterating the lettering, leaving a blank, flat panel.

On May 12, 1912, almost exactly eleven years to the date of filing his petition, Colonel James Ward Eddy, retiring at age 80, sold Angels Flight to the Funding Company of California. Though he was no longer the owner of the Flight, Colonel Eddy lived in the same neighborhood. His residence until he left Los Angeles in 1913 had been furnished rooms of the Hotel Hillcrest, 238 South Olive at the northeast corner of Third and Olive. During the nearly dozen years he owned the Flight, Eddy had lived within a stone's throw of his railway.

As a widower in 1900, he had married Jane Fisher Wiswell, who died one year after her husband's retirement. In 1913 Colonel Eddy moved to Eagle Rock, minutes away from Downtown Los Angeles. His new two-story bungalow, on the corner of West Colorado and Eddy Avenue, now El Rio, was close to daughter Carrie's residence. In 1915 Colonel Eddy's grand-daughter, Purle Gillette, married Herman Hensel in Eddy's home, where the young couple lived and cared for the aging Colonel.

As a Los Angeles resident, the Colonel had remained involved in civic-minded activities. Eddy was vice-president of the California Children's Home, president of the Los Angeles Orthopedic Hospital and a member of the Chamber of Commerce. In Eagle Rock he was one of the organizers of their Chamber of Commerce and served as a Vice President of the Eagle Rock Bank.

On Wednesday April 12, 1916, four years after his retirement, the original owner-operator of Angels Flight died. The weekly Eagle Rock paper reported that Eddy had been "Called Suddenly Hence." The cause of death was described as a "stroke of apoplexy," which had occurred the preceding Sunday. According to the Los Angeles *Times*, funeral services were held at the West Colorado residence of his daughter, Carrie Eddy Gillettte Sheffler. Interment was at the Hollywood Cemetery.

Colonel Eddy's estate, valued at $50,000, named his daughter Carrie as executrix. Distribution of his estate included the Colonel's gold watch, bequeathed to his grandson, Simeon Eddy Gillette. James Ward Eddy, the man whose unique railway had made such an impact on the lives of residents of Bunker Hill and the commercial world around it, left his own indelible print on the history of Los Angeles.

*Four generations: Colonel Eddy, daughter Carrie,
her son S. Eddy Gillette and his infant daughter. Circa 1906.*

Colonel J. W. Eddy,
owner-operator, 1901-1912.
Photo circa 1910,
courtesy Eddy family collection.

Robert M. Moore,
owner-operator, 1914 -1952.
Photo circa 1940, courtesy Moore
family collection.

Lester B. Moreland,
owner-operator, 1952 -1962.
Photo 1967, courtesy Moreland
family collection.

Chapter Five

Chain of Title

When the Funding Company of California purchased the popular funicular in 1912, the Los Angeles *Times* reported that Colonel Eddy was paid "$20,000 in cash, $20,000 in stock in the new company and $40,000 in bonds." Serving as the company's president, J. L. Christopher held 998 shares; H. C. Williams was vice-president with one share and Maynard Gunsel with one share was secretary-treasurer. Incorporation papers were filed by the Funding Company on November 11, 1912 with the name given as the Angels Flight Railway Company. Capital stock was listed as $100,000.

Just three days later a charter was issued by the State of California, which gave authority to operate a railway, known officially as Angels Flight. Previously the Flight had been classified by the City of Los Angeles as an electric elevator. Until the day it was dismantled, however, the funicular would retain both classifications. Under the State of California franchise, Angels Flight was operated as a railway and by permit of the City of Los Angeles it was operated as an electric elevator. The Funding Company had diversified plans in the electric railway field, but a singular accident, forced the untimely sale of Angels Flight.

Less than a year after the Funding Company of California had purchased Angels Flight, the only accident in the history of the incline railway occurred. The spectacular crash took place early Tuesday evening on the second day of September 1913. Details from the Los Angeles *Times* reveal that it was just after 6 p.m. and the Flight's operator, R. O. Dubois was in the power-house, his hand on the controlling lever, slackening the speed of the car (the Sinai) as it approached the top of the run.

The article reported that when the westward bound Sinai came within ten feet of its destination, sounds of the singular accident filled the air with strident discord. A four-inch steel control shaft had snapped. That shaft connected the hoist on the winch with the safety apparatus and the breaking of the steel control shaft loosened the cable which was hauling the Sinai to the station house. A cracking of steel, a roar of the cogs moving over the safety clutch, the rattling of the cable as it unwound from the spool added to the drama as the operator realized he could do little to stop the Sinai's slip to the bottom of the line.

The *Times* account spoke of fearful passengers looking anxiously to Dubois, who saw the stricken faces and heard the shrieks. Continuing to work his controls, the operator did manage to keep the car from going full speed on its backward slide toward the Hill Street archway where the Olivet was stopped. Only one passenger, George S. Biggin of Redlands, was reported on board that eastbound car when it halted, jerking slightly, just ten feet from the bottom. When Biggin looked up the incline and saw the Sinai on its shaky descent, he quickly jumped to safety.

According to the *Times*, the Sinai's 30 passengers, many returning home from work, were seconds away from disembarking when their car stopped momentarily, started back then careened downward accompanied by the jangle of ruined equipment. Striking its twin at the bottom of the run, the subdued Sinai rested at an angle, leaning in a southerly direction almost against the Ferguson Building at the corner of Third and Hill streets. While the Olivet had remained upright, the impact had rammed the car causing it to protrude through the archway and a few feet onto Hill Street.

There was one injury which could have been avoided. The *Times* reported that Mrs. William Hostetter, who had been sitting in one of the upper seats on the Sinai, decided to jump before the car reached the loop switch. The impulsive leap resulted in Mrs. Hostetter's being caught in a trestle. When the unfortunate woman was removed, she was carried up the incline to her residence at the Lovejoy Apartments on Third and Grand. The *Times* revealed that Mrs. Hostetter was then taken to Pacific Hospital where she was treated for internal injuries, a broken leg and broken collar bone.

A reporter, looking inside the awkwardly tilted Sinai, noted groceries, purses, shoes, hats and an enormous pineapple scattered in disarray. Because the speed of the car's descent had been kept in some measure of control by the hand of the Flight's operator, passenger injuries were largely bruises and sprains with few broken bones. A doctor and a lawyer were listed as injured passengers along with Mrs. Catherine Kimberley who was reported to have sustained a bruised thigh and facial cuts. Two months later Mrs. Kimberley, a milliner and Lovejoy Apartment neighbor of the injured Mrs. Hostetter, sued the Funding Company, seeking $40,000 in damages. Other suits were filed which led the Company into bankruptcy and its subsequent sale to Continental Securities in 1914.

Following the Flight's first and last accident, the State Railroad Commission requested the Funding Company to post notices to the effect that the Flight's equipment could not guarantee absolute safety to its passengers. Immediately, the owners took action to amend the problem areas. The rebuilt cars had devices installed to prevent their slipping down the incline; the shaft was replaced with a new and stronger one. That year the Mercereau Bridge and Construction Company did a partial reconstruction of the decking, added support bents of reinforced concrete and an extension of the length of the turn-out. Guard rails were placed along the outer part of each turn-out curve. When the railway was sold to the Continental Securities Company, brakes, automatic equipment and double glass further enhanced the safety features.

Olive Street Station House with view of the observation tower with camera obscura, 1920s. Courtesy Eddy family collection.

Barely two years after Colonel Eddy's sale to the Funding Company, title changed hands again when Robert M. Moore's Continental Securities purchased Angels Flight in 1914. In April of that year Mercereau Bridge and Construction Company filed a permit on behalf of the Angels Flight Railway Company to raise nine posts of the pavilion at the head of Angels Flight Incline at Third and Olive streets. Concrete was to be placed under the posts to raise them to their original level and the concrete floor under the pavilion was to be rebuilt. Cost of repairs was estimated at $500.

It was apparent that the land over the Third Street Tunnel was subsiding. In autumn of that year, on October 23, the Board of Public Works ordered the removal of Eddy's steel observation tower. Its structural stability in doubt from earlier years, the tower had begun to settle and list. Constructed on public land, the tower was in an area consisting of backfill in which the shoring timbers had not been removed. Rotting of those timbers caused voids in the soil and the subsequent listing of the tall tower. Nearly a quarter of a century would pass before Colonel Eddy's view tower with its camera obscura was finally removed. Visitors, however, were prohibited some time before it was taken down in 1938.

In the thirty-eight year stewardship of Robert M. Moore, there were two pedestrian accidents. Twenty-four years after the 1913 mishap, the Flight operator stopped the cars to investigate a jamming. What he found was a man who had taken a nap on the tram line. Jack Claus, reportedly a 54 year-old salesman, was severely injured when he was struck by the funicular on December 5, 1937. Six years later, in September 1943, a singular fatality occurred when a sailor heedlessly attempted to walk up the track and was crushed by one of the cars.

Robert M. Moore of Continental Securities had a background in mechanical engineering and a career in real estate and loans. Like Colonel Eddy, he had lived in Illinois and Arizona before arriving in Los Angeles. For thirty-two years Moore had presided as president and manager of the railway. By 1946 he was nearly 80 years old and in failing health. At that time Moore was ready to sell the Flight, but only to someone who would give devoted attention to the incline railway. Meanwhile, the decision was made to liquidate all the assets of his Continental Securities with the exception of the favored Angels Flight. As of October 16, 1946, Moore was listed as the Flight's owner. His nephew Walter H. Rankin was vice

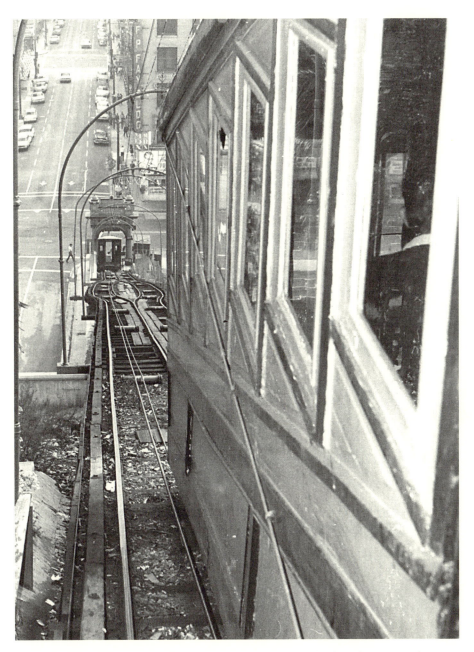

Angels Flight, with a hole in its window, offers a lovely ride six months before dismantling. Photo courtesy Eddy family Collection.

president and his younger brother Duncan Moore was secretary-treasurer. The assistant secretary was Mrs. I. M. Eskridge and the superintendent-operator was George Walker. According to a news account at that time, the City of Los Angeles offered to build an elevator and give Moore the deed if the City could tear down old Angels Flight. Moore would have no part of that plan.

For another six years Moore had the pleasure of running his beloved railway. In the summer of 1952, at the age of 85, he sold the popular attraction and retired. The following February he died at his home on 118 South Commonwealth Avenue, Los Angeles. Though Robert and Winifred Moore, who preceded him in death, had been childless, there were nine nieces and nephews in his family. Relatives and friends characterized Moore as gentlemanly and generous.

When Moore sold Angels Flight on August 23, 1952, he placed the railway in capable and caring hands. Lester B. Moreland and Byron Linville were the new owners. Again title change came quickly. Just six months after the purchase, Linville retired. On March 16, 1953, Moreland purchased Linville's interest in the Flight and the Moreland family took over running the railway. A retired electrical engineer, Lester Moreland became the president; Lester's father, Frank B. Moreland was the company's vice president and Lester's wife, Helen E. Moreland, was secretary-treasurer.

Lester Moreland's appreciation of Angels Flight began long before he made the decision to own the little railway. A native Californian who lived in Los Angeles' Silver Lake area, he had always known about Angels Flight and shared this mutual interest in conversations with his predecessor, Robert Moore. When Moreland worked in Downtown Los Angeles, he would park his car on Bunker Hill just so he could take Angels Flight enroute to his office at the Department of Water and Power on Third and Broadway. It was not only the pleasure of the brief ride, it was the entire concept of the funicular which appealed to Lester Moreland.

Lester's older son Robert and Robert's wife Barbara, who both grew up in the Silver Lake area, remember the family meeting which was called to discuss the possibility of buying Angels Flight. It was a bold and stunning idea, but very appealing. Being part of Angels Flight never lost its appeal to the Moreland family. Lester ran the business of the railway and

Helen Moreland took care of the complexities of the bookkeeping.
Their son Robert, who had his own career, helped to change the cables
and get the cars ready for the next day. This arrangement contributed to
keeping the railway on a financially solid base and helped to ensure that
there were no accidents during the Moreland stewardship.

Helen Moreland had been the Flight's historian and publicity
agent as well as the company's Secretary-Treasurer. In 1952, Helen,
who was a member of the Native Daughters of the Golden West,
Beverly Hills Parlor #289, was instrumental in having a bronze plaque,
commemorating 50 years of Flight operation, put on display at the
railway. As a background for the plaque a special drinking fountain had
been created.

On November 18, 1952, the bronze plaque, marking the first
formal recognition of Angels Flight, was dedicated and installed in the
pavilion area on the north side of the station house, facing Olive Street.
The well attended ceremony featured an unveiling of the plaque by Mayor
Flectcher Bowron and Los Angeles County Sheriff Eugene Biscailuz,
who lifted a California State flag to reveal the plaque with its drinking
fountain at the top of the small monument.

One of the speakers that November morning was S. Eddy
Gillette, the grandson who had inherited the Colonel's mechanical abilities
and his gold watch. Eddy, as he preferred to be called, died one month later
and was buried in the Colonel's family plot. Another speaker of historical
note was Miss Mary Emily Foy, who had been the first woman City
Librarian at the age of 18 in 1880. Miss Foy had lived in the home her
father built on Pearl Street (Figueroa). The Foy house was moved to
631 Witmer on Crown Hill in 1912. Declared Historic-Cultural
Monument No. 8 in 1962, the home has since been moved to the
more Victorian setting of Carroll Avenue on Angelino Heights.

Looking hale and vibrant at 90 years of age, Miss Foy told the
crowd that as a girl she would climb Bunker Hill, looking westward to
"that great lonely space, hill after hill." In the spring Mary Foy delighted
in picking the yellow violets which grew wild after a winter's rain. The
former librarian remembered seeing the tiny A. M. E. church founded by
Biddy Mason as well as a signal station where anyone with a spyglass
could see the ocean and ships coming to port.

Former Librarian Mary E. Foy speaks at the dedication of an Angels Flight commemorative ceremony on November 18, 1952. Courtesy Eddy family collection.

Throughout her association with the incline railway, Helen Moreland was a one-woman public relations team whose enthusiasm never waned. She gave lectures and slide shows on the background and foreground of Angels Flight. In 1956 Mrs. Moreland wrote a brief article on the railway for *Southland Motorist*. In 1959, she would tell the Los Angeles *Times* that she had ridden Angels Flight as a child on a visit to her teacher, who lived near the top of the railway. Later Helen helped to spearhead the nomination of Angels Flight for Historic Cultural Landmark designation.

In September of 1953, owner-operator Lester Moreland received an approval from the Los Angeles City Council to increase book fare prices from 50 rides for 50 cents to 30 rides for 50 cents. It was the first ticket book fare increase in the Flight's 51 year history. The single ticket remained five cents until the Flight was dismantled in 1969.

No one in the Moreland family was prepared for the precipitous end of their celestial railway. When Lester Moreland bought the Flight, he envisioned a long run for the electric incline. Equally disheartening to the Morelands was the leveling of everything on Bunker Hill. Having to sell their cherished railway was assuaged only slightly by the idea of its imminent return to the Hill. Seeing the venerable Angels Flight, after more than a quarter of a century in storage, easing up the eastern slope of Bunker Hill has been a vision the family savored.

When the franchise for the operation of Angels Flight expired on May 25, 1961, the City Council approved the extension for a one-year period pending redevelopment of Bunker Hill. The famous funicular was designated one of the six original Historic-Cultural landmarks in August of 1962. One month later the City Council approved an allocation of $35,000 by the Community Redevelopment Agency to purchase the Flight from Lester Moreland who had no other option except to sell. On October 16, 1962, escrow closed and the CRA took title to the property.

With that action, the nearly uninterrupted chain of personal ownership and operation of Angels Flight came to an end. Lester Moreland, like Robert Moore and Colonel Eddy before him had the enviable record of no railway accidents. One unifying thread connected owner-operators, James Eddy, Robert Moore and Lester Moreland: love of the little funicular and working knowledge of its function. No doubt the selfless time and

energy Colonel Eddy, Robert Moore and the Moreland family put into the
Flight's operation, invested the railway with its own enduring magnetism.

According to a column in the local *Downtowner*, "It was after the
Cultural Heritage Board, the American Institute of Architects and the
Native Daughters (of the Golden West) protested possible demolition of
the cable railroad that the City decided to acquire Angels Flight to guarantee its continuance." Subsequently Sidney J. Smith, vice president of
Oliver's & Williams Elevator Company, was named operator of the incline
railway until it ceased running in 1969. As the demolition and leveling of
Bunker Hill continued, fewer passengers climbed aboard the Olivet and the
Sinai, making the operation of the Flight a losing proposition for many
months. Revenues had dropped to $200 a month and operating expenses
were reported to be ten times that figure. In 1924, under the guidance of
Robert M. Moore as Manager, net revenues were $13,835.69, which
translates into $1,152.94 per month.

Smith's Elevator Company was assigned the task of dismantling
Angels Flight. According to Smith, the railway would need new cars
and virtually all new equipment. Like his predecessors, Sidney Smith
had formed a strong attachment to the railway, which was shared by
his wife Lillian, who had promised to keep an eye on the funicular
while it was in storage.

The chain of title remained static while the Flight languished in
storage for more than a quarter of a century. By the summer of 1995, it
was apparent that Bunker Hill Associates-California Plaza would not be
taking over the operation of Angels Flight. Filling that void was the Angels
Flight Operating Company, formed at the same time as the Angels Flight
Railway Foundation. Though Dennis Luna, a former CRA Commissioner
and the Foundation's chairman, initiated the AFRF, he credits the late
Jim Wood, a former CRA Chairman and union leader, with the original
suggestion. The Foundation came into being after the Angels Flight
Coordinating Committee had fulfilled its mission to oversee plans for the
restoration and return of the historic railway. When that project was successfully launched, the AFRF became the legal vehicle for fundraising and
operation of Angels Flight as well as having control of the ownership
of the Flight's assets and its museum collections.

In September, 1995, with the return of the historical landmark

A pigeon rests on the drinking fountain above the bronze plaque presented by the Native Daughters of the Golden West, Beverly Hills Parlor #289. Courtesy Graphic Arts, CRA.

only six months away, a memorandum from John E. Molloy, CRA Administrator, was issued to Community Redevelopment Agency Commissioners concerning "authorization to execute documents to effectuate operation of the Angels Flight Funicular Railway, Parcel Y-1, Bunker Hill Redevelopment Project." With City Council approval, the memorandum authorized the Agency's Administrator to assign the Angels Flight Railway Foundation (AFRF), a local non-profit, public benefit corporation, ownership of the Angels Flight Funicular Railway, historical monument and all construction and equipment warranties. The AFRF would lease the property on which Angels Flight operates and would have an adjacent Angels Flight Store and Angels Flight Museum.

The funicular and the store will be managed exclusively by the private Angels Flight Operating Company, John H.Welborne, president. A Los Angeles attorney, Welborne has been one of the most persistent voices for the return and restoration of the Flight, a regular attendee at committee meetings pertaining to that project, organizer of the fund-raising gala and events for the Flight's Re-Dedication and Re-Opening.

Legal complexities relating to Angels Flight's copyrights, trademarks and associated contracts were handled pro bono by Atlantic Richfield's Robert E. Lee. An attorney with expertise in intellectual property law, Lee worked with CRA attorney, Marcia Gonzalez-Kimbrough.

Transferring the chain of title from the Community Redevelopment Agency to the non-profit, community organization of the Angels Flight Railway Foundation gives the residents of the City of Los Angeles a closer tie with the contemporary Angels Flight.

Passengers wait to take a last ride on Angels Flight, May 1969.
Photo courtesy Julius Shulman.

Above: Interior of the Olivet with two layers of seats visible. Photo courtesy Doug Piburn. Right: Cutaway sketch by Ilma Cunningham.

Chapter Six

Inside-Out of Angels Flight

Standing on Bunker Hill that last day of 1901, celebrating the opening of his celestial railway, Colonel Eddy followed Mayor Snyder's
speech with one of his own concerning the safety of Angels Flight.
Eddy told the crowd that "Roebling and Sons, who made the cable, place
the breaking strain at 31,000 pounds. The weight of our car is 2700
pounds, to which add 2800 pounds possible live freight and we have 5500
pounds on a quarter-pitch grade, the equivalent of about 2700 on a vertical." He assured the gathering that though the strength of the cable
should be sufficient, if the working cable give way, another idle cable of
equal strength was ready to assume the burden. Eddy explained that this
safety principle applied to the brake as well, with the second brake coming
into use only if the first gave way.

Colonel Eddy further explained that the "goose neck" to which the
cable was attached, was necessary to carry the cable under the depression
pulley at Clay Street. It was made of wrought steel and was considered to be
even safer than the cable or the brake. His summary was brief, "Certainly
no one could be more desirous to have everything absolutely safe than
the builder, and it is his belief that this is so."

When Colonel Eddy made his first renovation of the Flight
in 1905, less than five years after the opening, new enclosed cars
had long narrow, louvered or vented windows. The Olivet
and Sinai, still a shade of white, continued
to symbolize Eddy's original
angelic concept. When
the enterprising

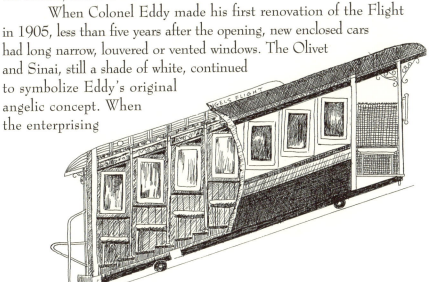

owner-operator made a major change to his incline railway, the *Southwest Contractor and Manufacturer*, March 26, 1910, stated that the respected architectural firm of Train & Williams had prepared plans, "for a one-story concrete pavilion, 50 x 17 feet . . . It will be classical design with open colonnades, one corner being enclosed for the power plant. There will be a terrace 9 feet wide on the west side. Cement floor, open-frame trussed roof covered with composition. A new track will be laid and new cars will be placed on the Flight." Leo Suck of 316 East Second Street had the contract for the cars and track. The one-story, ornate station house, rectangular in plan with a gable roof, was installed at the Olive Street summit, where an existing canopy had been removed.

City permit #3677 was filed on May 4, 1910, for Train and Williams by W. F. Klagas. The owner was listed as J. W. Eddy with his address whimsically given as "Angels' Flight City." The location of the building was described as "Facing Third Street at the top of Angels Flight on Olive Street." The purpose of the building was "Rest and R. R. Station." Dimensions were given as "16' x 6' x 47'-0." California Ornamental Brick Company was the contractor and the estimated cost was $3,000.

A description from the Historic Structures Report defines the archway. "Built as a free-standing element, it is composed of two columns with a cross canopy and ornamented arch infill around the canopy and a parapet above the columns. The parapet assembly is composed of two piers with a Neo-classical open balustrade located between them. The piers are capped with a composition of bell shaped domes and stepped horizontal planes. The finial detail of each dome features a mounting hole which held flagstaffs."

The prominent architectural firm of Train and Williams had designed the ornate arch and station house in keeping with the commercial Beaux Arts architecture of the city's downtown business buildings as well as Bunker Hill's Victorians. A description of the station house at the time of dismantling delineates the one-story building as being of "wood and concrete construction, one bay wide, the structure is of a wood frame placed inside a framework of cast stone columns and beams. Doric entabulature, Tuscan columns, stylized parapet, decorative classical ornamented surfaces and open arches represent the character-defining features of the

View of the Beaux Arts design archway, constructed in 1910.
Courtesy California Plaza.

station house. Constructed of hollow clay tile sheathed in stucco, the pavilion has more subdued detailing. In the 1920s a pavilion was added to replace the northern four bays of the original structure."

Sometime in the decade of the 1930s the cars were painted orange with black trim. There appears to be no historical documentation on the dramatic change of color, only speculation on the choice.

Notes from the Historic Resources Group describe the existing cars as having wood frame construction with wood siding and detailing. "Clad in canvas the wood frame roof is slightly arched. To accommodate the angle of the track, both the windows and cars are stepped. The series of seven windows corresponds to car bay division and seating layout. Seats are constructed of wood and there is decorative wrought iron trim at each end

Cluttered corner of the Station House, 1960s. Courtesy Graphic Arts, CRA.

of the vehicles." According to newspaper illustrations, the windows of the cars in 1911 were round. Remaining round for several years, the windows were later returned to the original rectangular shape.

Before Lester B. Moreland turned over Angels Flight to the CRA, he felt it incumbent upon himself to describe in detail the complete workings of the Flight and all its appurtenances. In a taped recording in 1962, he began, "This is L. B. Moreland speaking." From there the owner-operator of Angels Flight Railway meticulously explained everything from gears to gates, the trolleys, the motor, the brake system, safety and operation.

Like a thoughtful relative preparing a will, Moreland, in a style that mixes technical expertise and paternal commentary, explained that, "the motor pinion gear is four pitch and, I believe, 25 teeth, (and) drives the four pitch 114 tooth steel gear." It was his belief that, "the gears made by the Fisher Gear and Machine Company on South Santa Fe Avenue were quite satisfactory and priced reasonably." Moreland was just as explicit about having a safety gate which would not allow even one more passenger after the cars had started. The purpose was to keep patrons from running after the cars. "They are always in a hurry; they'd go up the track on crutches."

In speaking of the Westinghouse motor controller, Moreland explained that it was located in the control house and regulated the speed of the cars, the stopping, starting and reversing. He noted that the copper parts within the controller wore out about every six months and he advised having the controller checked "every month or so." Moreland described the motor as a 50 horsepower, three-phase, slip-ring operating on 480 volts at that time. The motor itself was bolted down to the floorplate, which was bolted on to concrete. "It is well," he suggested, "to check all the bolts from time to time because the vibration loosens them slightly."

Lester Moreland felt that "from an operating standpoint," the brake was the most important piece of equipment in the entire railway. He described the braking system as "the external contracting type" with the brake-shoes attached to iron bars anchored at the bottom of the pit and squeezed together against the brake drum at the top. The squeezing was done by a weighted arm. When the cars were started, the operator would lift the arm and hold the brake off. When the operator let go, the brake engaged automatically. The brake lining was one-half inch thick Johns Manville (asbestos), four and three-quarters inches wide.

Angels Flight engineer peers down the line, 1960s.
Courtesy Graphic Arts, CRA.

For the most part, the cables used on Angels Flight Railway were manufactured by John A. Roebling & Sons, whose firm, named for its founder John Augustus Roebling of Brooklyn Bridge fame, was the first in America to make wire rope. Moreland emphasized that it was "necessary to have the supplier furnish the cable to an exact length." The length of the main cable was 444 feet. Attached to the cars by means of turn buckles, a three-quarter inch safety cable measured 340 feet long. Cable inspection was made each morning by the rail operator and each week by the cable company. While the cable was adjusted for slack at least every three or four months, it was was changed approximately every 12 months. With the railway shut down about 11:00 p.m., it would take approximately 4 hours to make the complete change.

Moreland pointed out that the wheel bearings in the cars were special, having been cast from a pattern at the Fisher Brass Foundry in Vernon, California.

When Moreland took over the railway, the cars were showing their age, especially the floors. With over two million people a year stepping the terraced interior, the maple floors wore out rapidly and, according to Moreland, had a lifespan of about three years. In 1951 the floor had been changed, but Moreland realized that it was too expensive to buy floors. The work, tearing out the old and installing the new, would have to be done at night. He consulted with the M. T. A. and learned how they coped with wear from foot traffic.

Seventy-pound roofing paper was the answer and in 1953 it was installed in the cars with metal strips on the edgings of each step with Minnesota Mining and Manufacturing Company Safety Walk added for further protection against slipping. Moreland noted that nearly a decade later some of the roofing paper was the same as had been put there in 1953. Whenever a hole was worn in a step, it was immediately covered with the roofing paper.

At the time of Moreland's transfer of the railway, the seats were those which had been removed from Los Angeles Transit cars. Los Angeles Railway car seats were made of oak; the slats on the Flight's original seats were mahogany. Photos of the cars, taken during their warehouse duration, clearly show the two layers of seats with the oak over the mahogany. Moreland would say that there was never an opportunity to paint or varnish the seats because the drying time would be too costly.

The angled windows, which were double strength glass, were not immune from replacement. Rocks were thrown from the Clay Street alley; an inebriated passenger sometimes put an undisciplined elbow through the glass; suitcases or parcels were poked through the pane. A window broken with the car in motion was a major event causing operations to cease immediately. The operator was instructed to remove the glass and nail a plywood board, which was kept in the control house, over the window. This timely step was taken to prevent injury in the event someone put a hand out the open window. The California Glass Company replaced the windows at a cost of $13 each. Looking through those windows was just one diversion for Flight passengers; the other was reading advertisements posted on the walls above the windows in the style of a New York subway.

Canvas covered the roofs of the cars and Moreland admitted that the canvas had been deteriorating and was coming loose on the ends. It had been his practice to repaint the roofs at least once a year. They were covered with a special paint obtained from the people who had put the roofs on originally. When the company went out of business, Moreland was told that the "special" paint was regular house paint with a little more linseed oil added.

Repainting of the Olivet and the Sinai was done with Fuller Paint's Miratex. As expected, black for the trim, was called "Black" but the orange paint was called, "Danger Red." Painting the cars, whose measurements were 27'3" in length and 5'7" in width, was a night job which usually began at midnight.

Lester Moreland, as former steward of a beloved landmark, spoke at length on the importance of inspection of the railway and the choice of an operator of the Flight. Moreland felt that the operator was the most important man in the organization because he could literally "make or break the railway." It was his advice that an operator be in his fifties. Moreland felt that more mature operators were more stable in their activities and wouldn't be so inclined to leave after a short time. It was crucial not only that the safety of passengers be maintained, but also that gears not be broken by an inexperienced operator. Moreland estimated that the cost of repairing the large steel gear in the bottom of the pit, would probably have cost about $10,000 and shut down

The 9,000 lb. sheave in the station house. Sketch by Ilma Cunningham.

the railway from two to three weeks. In his taped report, Moreland went over the details of inspection, which included making a careful observation through the cars for signs of breakage or deterioration. He concluded with a modest reminder "look for any nails that might be sticking out enough to catch a passenger's clothing."

Angels Flight of Moreland's day ran on a 30-inch gauge line, made of 40 pound iron. Rather than a switching system to allow passage of the cars, the Flight had a three-rail system with a four-rail passing bay, mid-way along the tracks.

Hill Street was the entrance most frequented by patrons of the Flight even though the fare box, mechanical systems and attendant were all housed at the top of the incline. The all-important operator was in complete control of the loading of passengers at this station where a single one-bar gate handled the traffic. The lower station had to be remotely controlled. Following the railway's single accident of 1913, an electrically operated turnstile had been installed, preventing late passengers from boarding the moving cars. There was another measure of safety in a notice posted on the cars themselves. Just below a red caution sign, the notice read: "DO NOT ENTER CAR AFTER SOUND OF HORN or WHEN RED LIGHT IS ON."

When the operator decided it was time to start the car, a button was pressed, a klaxon horn sounded and a red warning light came on. The operator would look down the track through the open-ended cars to make certain all was clear. At the top there was a bell which was rung to warn passengers that the car was going to move. It was a signal to take a seat or grab on to one of the vertical poles. Power was applied to the motor and Angels Flight was off and running. Cruising at just under 4 miles per hour, the Olivet and Sinai covered their block-long course in less than 50 seconds, making about 400 trips each day, beginning at 6:00 a. m. and running until 12:20 a.m.

*Olive Street entrance to Angels Flight, Spring 1969.
Photo courtesy Julius Shulman.*

Artist Leo Politi painted a reverie of imagination of early Bunker Hill and Angels Flight. Courtesy Leo Politi family.

Chapter Seven

The Hill and The Flight in Retrospect

Don Ryan, a reporter for the Los Angeles Times in the 1920s, was a frequent rider of Angels Flight. Capturing the atmosphere of Bunker Hill, his novel *Angel's Flight* was published in 1929. The author's fictional alter ego is a reporter who rides the cable car which, "landed him above the tops of the brittle palms and loquat trees. On the cracked concrete invalids were sunning themselves in wheelchairs along the railway where they could see the city below." Not stopping to watch by the rail, the reporter climbs the steel tower's long flight of steps to Colonel Eddy's camera obscura for a view of "Los Angeles . . . inflating itself to a degree that it shall be reckoned the largest city in the world." Musing as he views "a living map of Los Angeles," the reporter makes a laundry list of the city's assets, linking such diversities as ostriches, oranges, alligators, olives, bungalows, casabas, snowy peaks and pepper trees.

In the early 1930s, author John Fante lived on Bunker Hill at the Alta Vista Hotel, writing and working as a waiter to support himself. In his novel *Ask The Dust* (1939) Fante caught the mood of Bunker Hill and the deteriorating neighborhood. "I walked down Olive Street past a dirty yellow apartment house . . . past horrible frame houses reeking with murder stories."

Writing those murder stories, Raymond Chandler used the faded Victorian elegance and run-down twentieth century neglect as background for novels such as *The High Window* (1942). His novel's detective, Philip Marlowe describes Bunker Hill of the '40s "lost town, shabby town, crook town . . . cokies and coke peddlers; people who look like nothing in particular and know it." Chandler's view of the apathy of those inhabitants of Bunker Hill is graphically detailed. "In the tall rooms haggard landladies bicker with shifty tenants. On the wide, cool front porches . . . sit the old men with faces like lost battles."

Author-illustrator Leo Politi, a long-time resident of Bunker Hill, sketched and painted the once grand mansions, saving them for posterity with his inimitable artistry. *Bunker Hill, Los Angeles: Reminiscences of Bygone Days* (1964) contains some of the paintings of Politi's Bunker Hill collection along with stories of the Hill dwellers who knew their link with a gracious past was about to be severed.

Pensioners enjoying a once-proud Victorian at 246 S. Bunker Hill Ave., 1950s. Photo T. S. Hall, courtesy Huntington Library.

Author-illustrator Leo Politi sketching, 1950s. Photo courtesy Leo Politi family.

Like Chandler, Leo Politi saw "the old men with faces like lost bat-tles," but Politi also saw the soft edges of those twilight years of Bunker Hill. By the 40s and 50s life on the Hill was worlds away from the air of wealth and elegance of the late 1880s, yet it had its own graceful moments with pensioners tending their flowers or sitting on their porches with sleeping cats.

Piccolo's Prank (1965), one of Politi's stories for children, is filled with drawings of Angels Flight and Bunker Hill with its rooming house-mansions, caught in a time suspension. The artist's richly detailed illustrations open a long-closed window on the ebbing years of the Hill's neighborhood. A two-page illustration catches a moment, vibrant with life, a scene of Angels Flight and a vignette of activities on the hilltop. Angels Flight is poised at a breath-taking angle which offers a view of the old Metropolitan Water office and the Grand Central Market. On the

In The Glenn Miller Story, Jimmy Stewart is on Bunker Hill with Angels Flight in the background. 1953 film clip, courtesy Library of Moving Images.

hill children at play run through the streets, an elderly man with a cane walks gingerly. A block away a crane dangles a wrecking ball.

Angels Flight and environs caught the attention of Hollywood and made appearances in films as well as books. Everything about the unique railway invited filming: proximity to the Third Street tunnel, the unusually ornate arch and station house at the bottom and top of the Flight, the Olivet and Sinai themselves with their strangely angled windows and haunting Halloween colors, the sounds of the funicular as it toiled up the track, that scraping and whining; the klaxon horn at start of the run. At the top of the Flight were the old Victorians and views of the city below, all tailor-made for filming.

The Unfaithful, a film starring Ann Sheridan, offered a look at Bunker Hill and Angels Flight in the 1940s. Columbia Pictures' early 1950's American version of "M" shows the villain hurrying his intended victim past the Hill Street entrance of Angels Flight. Actors included

David Wayne, Howard DaSilva and Raymond Burr. In 1952 William Holden was featured in *The Turning Point,* a film in which the actors shuttle up and down Angels Flight until a dramatic moment at the Olive Street station house. *The Glenn Miller Story*, a 1953 production, shows Jimmy Stewart on Bunker Hill looking for a trombone in a pawn shop across from Angels Flight. A 1956 Lon Chaney movie had a dramatic scene on the railway.

Deane Romano's screenplay for a murder mystery, *Angel's Flight*, was filmed on Bunker Hill in 1962. The haunting theme song of the film's title is sung by Ann Richards, former wife of jazz great Stan Kenton. Making a brief appearance in this film noir is actress Rue McClanahan. Daytime and nighttime views of Angels Flight shortly before its dismantling and scenes of Bunker Hill just before its demolition document those last years of the Hill and the Flight.

In 1956 the University of Southern California's film school made a documentary simply titled, "Bunker Hill, 1956," which starkly portrays the pensioners, their use of Angels Flight and their unique community on Bunker Hill. Edmund Penney's brief, but powerful documentary, *Angel's Flight,* (1964) caught an aging funicular as it heroically continued its run while bulldozers and a 3000 pound wrecking ball leveled the hilltop. TV's *Boston Blackie* series occasionally used the railway as background and there had been a live theatre production of a play with the name of the famous funicular.

Writers wove the Flight and vignettes from Bunker Hill into their works; Hollywood offered glimpses of the famous funicular carrying passengers with famous faces. Artists, particularly Ben Abril and Leo Politi painted scenes of Angels Flight and mansions on the Hill. Photographers, notably Arnold Hylen, William Reagh, and former Bunker Hill resident Theodore Hall, visually preserved much of all that is left of the hill's historic architecture. A Millard Sheets painting of the Flight is on display at the Los Angeles County Museum of Art and an original Angels Flight scene by the late primitive painter, Streeter Blair, is in Downtown's Los Angeles Chamber of Commerce building.

Another record of the incline railway can be found in voices from old Bunker Hill, voices of riders of Angels Flight. Mildred Moody had worked in Downtown Los Angeles in the 1920s as an artist at Barker

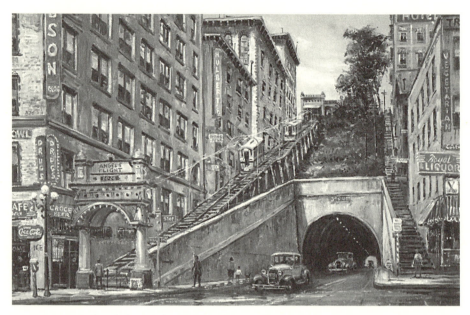

Angels Flight in the 1930s. Photo of a painting by Ben Abril.

Brothers where she did rosemaling, the art of decorating furniture with flowers, birds and ornate scrolls. For one memorable assignment Mildred painted flowers and gold scroll on a white grand piano. The special detailing was requested by Los Angeles' popular preacher, the vibrant Aimee Semple McPherson. Walking from her downtown studio at Barker Brothers, Miss Moody rode Angels Flight to her rooming house on Bunker Hill. At the time, Bunker Hill offered low rents, a safe haven for young ladies and the pleasure of the Flight's step-saving ride with its economical 5 cent fare.

Of the many who have known the pleasure and usefulness of riding "the shortest railway in the world," Leonard Bernstein, proprietor of antiquarian books at the Caravan Book Store on South Grand, has vivid memories. He recalls youthful excursions with his mother during the Christmas season when Angels Flight was magically lit. On weekends the family would park on Olive Street and take the Flight to the Downtown area where the wings of Pegasus, Mobile Oil Company's flying horse logo, flared in crimson neon. Along Sixth Street offices of steamship lines displayed model ships with light streaming from the portholes. As a boy Leonard was fascinated with the engineering and mechanics of the little railway, an enduring interest revealed in the miniature trains which ornament his book store.

Tracy Lyon, whose family once owned the Grand Central Market, begins his recollection of Angels Flight at the age of four. From the vantage point of the Market on Hill Street, he watched as a small train went up what appeared to be a mountain. A short time later Tracy had his first ride on the Flight. Like scores of young passengers, he stood by his father in the exterior seat for better viewing and like those young riders, Tracy remembers the rush of adrenalin when the cars appeared headed for collision. By the time he was eight, the magic of the little funicular had worked its spell and Tracy was hurrying across Hill Street with his nickels to take exciting rides solo up and down the block-long track. Later as a young man he watched the inexorable changes on the Hill and the dismantling of the Flight. Tracy realized that an important connection not only to Grand Central Market but to Bunker Hill and its past had been severed.

This loss of connection between the Historic Core and old Bunker Hill, two sibling neighborhoods, was recognized by The Yellin Company, present owners of Grand Central Market, which sees the restored Angels Flight as both a symbolic and a functional reconnection. The Historic Core, a reflection of the city's diverse ethnic character, is defined by the Yellin Company as an emerging governmental center whose linkage with Bunker Hill's financial and cultural focus will give Downtown unity, vitality and visual excitement.

Photographing Bunker Hill in the 1950s and 1960s, Arnold Hylen thought Bunker Hill Avenue, lost in the urban renewal leveling along with Clay and Cinnebar streets, may have represented the very essence of the Hill. Hylen referred to the Avenue, running parallel to Grand between Grand and Hope, as "a unique little world."

Beverly Moore would agree with that concept. As a young girl in the early 1940s Beverly Beaumont Moore lived with her family at 255 Bunker Hill Avenue in the Alta Vista apartments, an imposing five-story white structure, flanked by a pair of long Corinthian columns. With Rose Marie Caulfield, her best friend and neighbor at 311 Bunker Hill Avenue, Beverly would spend a nickel for a ride down Angels Flight to Broadway, which literally sparkled with ornate movie palaces.

Alta Vista Apts., 225 S. Bunker Hill Ave., 1950s. Photo by T. S. Hall, courtesy Huntington Library.

Million Dollar Theatre on S. Broadway with announcement of its opening day,
February 1, 1918. Courtesy The Yellin Company.

Ferguson Building, 1940. Eddy's observation tower is gone and the B. P. O. E. letters on the archway have been filled in flush with the panel. Photo T. S. Hall, courtesy Huntington Library.

The Million Dollar Theatre looked exactly that. For just ten cents they could see the latest double feature and on occasion one of the stars of the film in a personal appearance.

Heading back to their Bunker Hill Avenue homes, the girls would pass the eight-story Ferguson Building, completed in 1911 on the southwest corner of Third and Hill streets at the foot of Angels Flight. There was nothing about this unassuming structure to indicate that its architect, George Herbert Wyman, was the same man who designed the ethereal Bradbury Building, just one block down on the southeast corner of Third and Broadway. Wyman was a young draftsman when he designed the peerless Bradbury; the Ferguson was indicative of his style after certification as an architect.

Beverly remembers the Bunker Hill Avenue neighborhood with no graffiti, no trash littering the tree-lined streets. It was a safe and pleasant place, typical of most small towns of that era, where she walked without fear. A vacant lot on Olive was used by the neighborhood youth as their own sports park for ball games and recreation. Like many neighborhood communities there were small shops: dry cleaners, shoe repair, markets, including a deli at Third and Grand and an Italian store on Olive Street as well as a drug store with a popular soda fountain.

Beverly Moore moved away before she was an adult but she never forgot the Hill or Angels Flight and finds it difficult to reconcile those tranquil years in a closely knit neighborhood with the grandeur of the skyscrapers commanding the Hill today.

By the early 1950s sleazy commercial establishments made an appearance at the bottom of Bunker Hill. Frank Leslie Mapson was staying at the Fremont Hotel, which welcomed the young actor and his dog Magnolia. A short walk to the Biltmore Theatre, originally located in the northwest corner of the hotel, brought Mapson from Third Street past the neon bright burlesque houses on Hill Street.

As grandchildren of owner-operator Lester Moreland, Nancy and Greg Moreland had the unique pleasure of growing up with Angels Flight in their family. Most of their youthful birthday parties had some involvement with the incline railway. One of Nancy's earliest remembrances includes the organ grinder and his monkey, as portrayed in Politi's *Piccolo's Prank*. Seeing the artificial fruit and flowers on Nancy's straw purse, the monkey would attempt to remove them.

Lester Moreland enjoyed showing his little granddaughter how the railway worked and Nancy enjoyed being inside the station house where the operator commanded the Olivet and the Sinai on their up and down runs. A favorite run of Nancy's was to try to beat the upward bound car to the top of Olive Street. She would race up the 120-odd steps time after time until she was successful; then she stopped racing the funicular.

Nancy's brother, Greg grew up to be a mechanical and lighting engineer with the same affection and enthusiasm for Angels Flight as his engineer grandfather. Although he was a young boy when Lester Moreland was in charge of the Flight, Greg has clear and poignant memories about those times with his grandfather. Like his sister Nancy, Greg remembers being shown time and again how things worked on the little railway. His grandfather was rewarded when young Greg noticed a roller which wasn't working. Greg knows now that in the guise of taking his young grandson on the Flight to go shopping or for lunch, the elder Moreland would actually be observing the operator and the Flight's operation. With his interest in lighting alive even as a youth, Greg recalls the interior lighting of the Olivet and Sinai and arched poles with Christmas bells in season. Greg remains impressed with the fact that his Grandfather wanted all of his family members to be paying passengers. Even though Lester Moreland might give the money to his young grandson for a ride, it was important that he be treated the same as the other paying passengers. No free rides.

In a rich mosaic entwining Angels Flight, pensioners and overwrought
Victorian architecture, artist Frank L. Mapson's abstract captures the
essence of Bunker Hill's ebbing years.

ANGELS FLIGHT

Will temporarily discontinue service as of 10:30 p.m., Sunday, May 18, 1969. Angels Flight will be disassembled and stored until the time when the top of Bunker Hill has been graded. It is hoped that this will take no longer than two years. Then Angels Flight will be reassembled in this same location. To mark the temporary closing, there will be a brief ceremony, Friday, May 16, at 12:30 p.m.

All passengers may ride free the last weekend.

Schedule of free rides:

Friday, May 16: 1:00 p.m. to 10:30 p.m.
Saturday, May 17 and
Sunday, May 18 7:00 a.m. to 10:30 p.m.

THE COMMUNITY-REDEVELOPMENT AGENCY
CITY OF LOS ANGELES

Sketch of CRA notice posted at Angels Flight, 1969.
Ilma Cunningham, Artist.

Chapter Eight

Demolition/Dismantling

At the turn of the nineteenth century business enterprises and the Civic Center were located below the city's main promontory while the social life of Los Angeles centered on Bunker Hill. Prominent residents included merchants, physicians, lawyers, bankers, politicians, some of whom left a definitive mark on the history of Los Angeles. Angels Flight, and to a lesser extent Court Flight, carried passengers to and from the parties, ceremonies and other social events on the Hill.

Change, however, was endemic in the burgeoning City of Angels and by 1910 the Los Angeles *Times* described Main Street as "a mixture of skyscrapers and hovels." Soon progress would taint even the Elysian heights of Bunker Hill. Economic development around Broadway brought commercial buildings up onto the Hill in the form of both multi-family apartments and business structures. The Crocker mansion, on the south side of Angels Flight terminus, had become a boarding house; the Hotel Hillcrest anchored the northeast corner of Third and Olive.

Viewpoints on the value of Bunker Hill varied widely since its earliest development. In the spring of 1874, Los Angeles *Star* editor Major Benjamin C. Truman, complimented Prudent Beaudry for demonstrating with his construction of reservoirs that the fertility of the mesa lands of Bunker Hill was a blessing to the community "by relieving them of the curse of sterility." A similar compliment was given to Colonel Eddy in the Los Angeles *Herald* of January 1, 1902. Reporting on the opening ceremony of Eddy's "novel enterprise," the article described the mayor's speech "in the happiest vein" speaking of the appreciation of the miniature railway for "beautifying the rough and unsightly face of the hill."

By 1929 voices were clamoring for the removal of Bunker Hill, its fertility and all. One of the loudest voices belonged to C. C. Bigelow, president of the Southwestern Investment Corporation. It was his opinion that the tunnels which had been bored through the expansive hill served only to relieve traffic congestion, while furthering the isolation of the hill area itself. His blunt and specific proposal was to remove twenty million cubic yards of earth, thereby razing the hill. Bigelow believed that "Bunker Hill has been a barrier to progress in the business district of Los Angeles, preventing the natural expansion westward . . . If this Civic Center is to be a

success, the removal or regrading of Bunker Hill is practically
a necessity."

With that prediction in mind William Babcock and Son,
Engineers prepared a plan two years later. This alternate plan would have
massively regraded but not razed the hill. It was the engineering firm's suggestion that the land be acquired by a central owner for the project.

There were yet other voices, beckoning westward, luring a second
generation of wealthy Bunker Hill residents. W. W. Robinson in his research
on the "Southern California Real Estate Boom of the Twenties," describes
the 25 to 30 land lookers who would enjoy the bus ride and
lunch, courtesy of a land broker, who spoke with animation as the bus rolled
down Wilshire Boulevard, "In the distance you will see the large sign of
Hollywoodland, the Wilshire Country Club . . . Hawaiian palms . . .
brought over here at great expense . . . Buy property like this and keep it,
and as sure as the world moves, it will pay you one hundred per cent to
one thousand per cent."

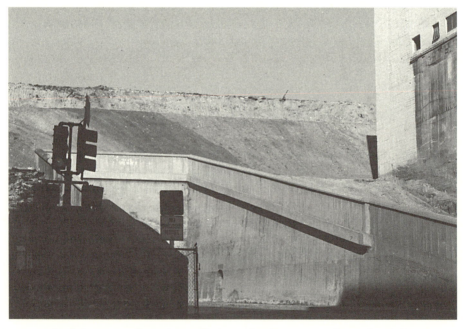

A leveled section of Bunker Hill above the former site of Angels Flight in
November 1969. Courtesy Eddy family collection.

In 1929, joining Silverwoods on the Miracle Mile, Bullocks-Wilshire Department Store opened at 3050 Wilshire Boulevard, attracting affluent customers with its Moderne design, superb Art Deco interior and a new feature, off-street parking. Auto parks made an appearance in 1934 on Bunker Hill, covering former residential sites. By the mid-1940s the Hill's Victorian elegance had definitely faded. Though there were still solid old mansions with architectural grace notes of another era, the Hill was beginning to wear a down-at-the-heels look and the inexorable march toward demolition continued.

In a compendium of studies, *Los Angeles: Preface to a Master Plan*, urban experts concluded: "Bunker Hill is not a detriment to the downtown area; it is an asset. It supplies excellent sites for superior types of multiple dwellings commanding a view of the entire surrounding country. Such structures would provide replenishment of the downtown tributary resident purchasing power, which is urgently needed, and encourage the rehabilitation of nearby blighted areas." The findings of the urban experts may have been a collective voice of reason crying in the wilderness.

From 1947 to 1952 Henry Luna, now retired, worked as an architect for the County of Los Angeles in the architectural division of the engineering department. At that time Luna was working with the City Estimator on Bunker Hill. Specifically the work site was county land from First to Temple streets and Broadway to Hope, where the Music Center is today. Luna recalls the fact that 1.5 million cubic yards of dirt were removed in the grading of that area. The majority of material removed was used for the building of the San Bernardino Freeway.

In a 1958 article for *Western City*, Joseph Bill, then Executive Director of the Community Redevelopment Agency (CRA), spoke of Bunker Hill's urban renewal as being the largest and most dramatic in the United States. Bill wrote that the city "needs a strong heart to nourish its sprawling body." It was his opinion that human scale and beauty would be the keynotes of the new "city within a city."

The CRA acquired its first land on Bunker Hill when the Agency purchased three run-down rooming houses for $68,000 in the spring of 1961. By May of the following year, Yukio Kawaratani began his work on the Bunker Hill Project as City Planner for the CRA. For over three decades Yukio would pursue the Agency's goal to make downtown Los

339 S. Bunker Hill Ave., circa 1968. The "Salt Box House,"
Historic Cultural Monument #5. Courtesy Urban Archives CSUN.

Angeles the rightful office center of the region with Bunker Hill as the focal point. In the 1960s Downtown had government buildings, but Wilshire Boulevard was the private office center of the region. According to Kawaratani, Bunker Hill could not boast of a single office building at that time. The former Principal Planner stated that in order for the CRA to prepare the Hill for high density development, it was necessary to cut the top of the hill and then construct a multi-level street system.

The CRA's Director of Engineering, Jerry Gross, had a long term connection with Bunker Hill. In his teens he worked at a Richfield gas station on Fourth and Flower streets when Bunker Hill was in its days of decline. Gross pointed out that prior to the Hill's demolition, an area between Fifth and Fourth Streets had been solid parking lots. According to Gross a number of buildings had outlived their usefulness and the land was more valuable. He emphasized that there was economic pressure for urban redevelopment and he believed that left to its own devices, development on the Hill would have been "hodge-podge."

In December of 1963, after the Morelands' sale of the incline railway, the decision was made to change the hours of the Flight's operation. The reduced schedule began at 7 a.m. and ended at 10:30 p.m. It was noted that there were less than 10 riders between the hours of 10 p.m. and 12 a.m. and there was a feeling that closing down before midnight would be less dangerous for the lone operator in the wheel-house. However, two years later the *Herald Examiner* carried the story of a robbery at the Flight's station house one spring evening with the loss of $170.

While the Flight's ridership was declining, the net rental income to the CRA from all acquired parking lots in the project as of June 30, 1963 was $242,784.

A press release from the Los Angeles Municipal Arts Department, dated May 21, 1969, just three days after the closing of Angels Flight, crystallized the Community Redevelopment Agency's rationale for erasing the architectural and community elements of an era in Downtown Los Angeles' history. Titled "Angel's Flight Hibernation," the release stated, "Temporary removal of Angel's Flight was necessary to permit the CRA to proceed with its multi-million-dollar urban renewal master plan. When completed, within the next decade, Bunker Hill will be the vital center of downtown Los Angeles."

Watching the slow decline and swift fall of Bunker Hill, photographer Arnold Hylen voiced his lamentations about its passing in *Bunker Hill, A Los Angeles Landmark* (1976). Hylen noted that for the first half of the twentieth century, Bunker Hill, "continued almost unnoticed by any except its nondescript population and, of course, by developers and some planners whose dreams and schemes eventually sealed its doom."

In his book *Los Angeles: The Enormous Village* (1980), John Weaver summed up the abandoning of Bunker Hill "by men who had grown old and rich buying, selling, lending and speculating, healing and suing. Moving westward toward the sea, they flung up French chateaux and English manor houses on the recycled beanfield of Beverly Hills. The Gothic mansions of their childhood were left to a mixed lot of pensioners, prostitutes and petty criminals."

Of the "mixed lot" described by Weaver, and the "nondescript population," described by Hylen, as many as nine thousand were senior citizens who relied on Angels Flight with its five-cent ride to shuttle them down to Hill Street and back. The Flight served as a valuable link from the Hill to the city below. Grand Central Market and a Good Will Industries were there with affordable prices; Pershing Square, a short two blocks south, offered an opportunity to play chess, engage in discussions or just sit in the sun on one of the benches.

The eighteen-minute documentary, "Bunker Hill 1956," made by the University of Southern California Film Department, graphically captures that point in time. Three male resident senior citizens, a doctor, a pharmacist and a carpenter, speak of life on Bunker Hill in their declining years. With one voice their message clearly described the pleasure and the convenience of living in an affordable residential neighborhood on the fringe of downtown. The men pointed out what a good feeling it was to be in a community where everyone knew his neighbor; everyone had a sense of dignity and independence. One senior said that on Bunker Hill they could still "take part in the business of living." They walked the neighborhood without fear and sat with their peers on benches in a small hillside park overlooking the Civic Center. In addition to the spouses of the men, there were scenes of women, sculpting and painting in their apartments, pleased to be independent in their own spaces. They spoke of their despair of the time when they would have to leave Bunker Hill. Those senior pensioners were a part of Bunker Hill's community and Angels Flight was the artery connecting them with the city.

Steep and formidable, Bunker Hill was described by sociologists at the end of the 1930s as having a population of low income, low occupation and heavily weighted with older men. Run-down and pensioner-populated, with only 2.2 per cent of the dwellings owner occupied, it was still Downtown's only communal heartbeat. There was a thriving nightlife on the Hill with cafes, restaurants and nightclubs. From its days of social glitter and magnificent mansions at the turn of the century to the pace of the pensioners and faded rooming houses in the twentieth century, Bunker Hill had been a unique and distinctive residential community. Writing in his Los Angeles *Times* column in 1964, Art Siedenbaum commented on the 315 feet of Angels Flight as measuring the distance between community and city.

*224 S. Olive typified homes which were considered part of a social blight
in the Bunker Hill neighborhood circa 1959. Photo T. S. Hall,
courtesy Huntington Library.*

A child stands on a fine, old bench to scribble on a board covering a vestige of Victorian elegance in a Bunker Hill mansion, 1960s.
Courtesy Graphic Arts, CRA.

Like Bunker Hill the future of Angels Flight had been threatened years before the end came. On June 6, 1935, the City Council proposed to terminate the franchise of the railway ostensibly to widen the stretch of Third Street from the tunnel entrance to Hill Street. Twelve hundred residents and other friends of the railway protested the change and local papers took up the story. Rejecting the plan to widen the tunnel, the City Council granted a ten-year extension of the Angels Flight franchise.

Undisturbed for nearly a quarter of a century, the Olivet and Sinai continued counterbalancing their passenger loads, totaling over 100 million riders in the first fifty years. As early as 1948 an impending shadow was cast over the future of the landmark funicular when the City Council declared the need for a Redevelopment Agency. According to Don Parsons, architect and urban planner, initial proposals by the Community Redevelopment Agency to redevelop Bunker Hill called for land use which was "predominantly residential." It would include" the construction principally of limited-height elevator apartment buildings so spaced and oriented as to take full advantage of views, sun and breeze." Three years later fifteen areas in the city were designated as blighted, listing Bunker Hill Central Redevelopment Area No. 1.

In 1953 voters saw the defeat of public housing and the election of Norris Poulson as mayor. Five years later a front-page article in the Los Angeles *Times*, titled "Big Bunker Hill Project Wins Approval of U. S.," presented a photo of Los Angeles Mayor Poulson, U. S. Senator from California, Thomas Kuchel, and Federal Housing Administrator, Albert M. Cole. As Administrator of the Housing and Home Finance Agency, Cole was putting his signature of approval on the huge urban renewal plan for Bunker Hill. The loan figure was $57,504,203 of which $15,469,203 would ultimately become an outright grant. Mayor Poulson commented, " We are proposing to spend money and put people to work on something we need and ought to have, something that represents a sound investment in better living, better business and a better community."

In March 1959, the City Council passed an ordinance mandating a Bunker Hill project. In October of that same year issuance of $20,000,000 in bonds by the Agency had been authorized. It was the conclusion of city officials that the once fashionable neighborhood of Victorian-era homes and buildings had deteriorated and constituted a social blight, fostering crime and fire hazards. A Los Angeles Department of Health survey in 1955 had

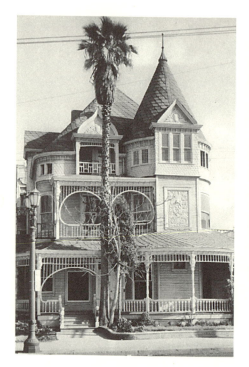

*Richelieu Hotel, S. Grand Ave. Photo on left indicates the appearance
of the hotel until the day of its demolition, photo on right, in 1957.
Photos T. S. Hall, courtesy Huntington Library.*

found only 18 percent of the units on Bunker Hill acceptable for
habitation; 20 percent were termed poor, 22 percent substandard and
40 percent extremely undesirable.

Two years later a Building and Safety Department report noted
60 percent of the structures dangerous with 16 percent substandard.
Adding fuel to the demolition rationale was a report of the crime rate,
which was double the city average with a high incidence of narcotics
addiction. Clearly redevelopment forces wanted to level the Hill for economic progress; a case was made for blighted conditions on Bunker Hill;
the historic Victorians were in need of repair or in total disrepair; age
and wood construction of the large homes made them fire hazards.

The Dome, a Turkish style 67-unit hotel with a red tile roof and turret was gutted by fire on July 24, 1964. Equally to the point was the fact that a height limitation on the site had kept new construction off the hill.

In spite of mounting evidence provided by the city, which appeared to favor a drastic change on the Hill, there were homeowners on the Hill, preservationists and other concerned citizens who had hopes for salvaging some of the best of the Victorians, preserving landmarks and establishing some kind of community which would combine the residential with business in the central city. Bunker Hill property owners did take legal action to block clearance and the rebuilding of the Hill. In 1961, however, the city won a favorable decision, which was later upheld by the California State Supreme Court

Long before the Flight was dismantled, there were discussions in 1962 about the fate of the popular funicular. While a clear decision had not been made by the CRA, it was thought that the railway might be kept where it was with limited use as the area would change; eventually there would be no need for the little incline. Later plans and speculations about the future of the funicular were noted In the Los Angeles *Times* when it was reported that "the Community Redevelopment Agency plans to tear it (Angels Flight) down, store it, refurbish it and put it back together again on the same hillside to serve Bunker Hill's new generation of office workers and residents." The article continued with the belief that "the railway would be out of commission one and one-half to two years while engineers smooth off the top of Bunker Hill for the renewal area's new street pattern." At that same time it was argued that the Flight's turn-of-the century features would be incongruous in the glittering realm of high-rise apartments and skyscrapers.

At the southern end of Bunker Hill, the first land sale came in 1965. South Figueroa, between Fourth and Fifth streets, was the site of the first building of the urban renewal project, the 42-story Union Bank Square. With a view unimpeded by buildings, Angels Flight continued to make its way up and down the incline whose borders were becoming more desolate with each passing day. Seven days a week, the Olivet and the Sinai continued their runs. Passengers on the Flight were fewer and fewer as demolition leveled building after building.

95

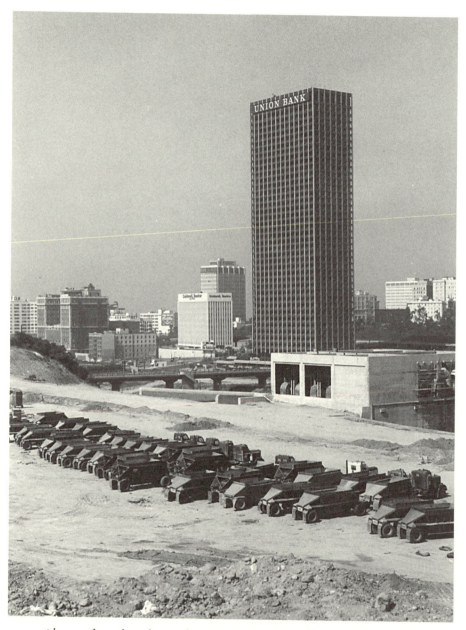

Above: Fleet of trucks used to regrade Bunker Hill, September 1969.
Photo courtesy Eddy family collection.

Top right: D. F. Donegan residence, 325 S. Bunker Hill Ave., 1950s. Courtesy California Plaza. Bottom right: Ill-fated Donegan "Castle" cut in sections to be moved to Heritage Square, 1969. Courtesy Graphic Arts, CRA.

Art Deco splendor of the Richfield Building razed to build ARCO Plaza in 1969. Photo 1930s, courtesy ARCO Photographic Department.

Meanwhile a fleet of trucks hauled dirt from Bunker Hill as fill for Los Angeles freeways such as the Artesia in Lakewood. The *Times* reported in an article written just days before the dismantling of Angels Flight that "eight square blocks would be lowered and contoured to make the hilltop more saleable and useable." The $960,000 excavation-grading job changed the Hill's profile and reduced sharp grades on Grand Avenue and Second Street which had ranged from 16 to 24 percent. It was reported that Grand Avenue was lowered forty feet.

Riding Angels Flight in 1967 presented an ironic experience. The charming old funicular climbed up an historic hill which was visibly and audibly being eaten away by the wrecking ball and bulldozers. When the area was finally cleared by the CRA, the land was divided into parcels to be sold separately to developers for a variety of offices, condominiums and high-rise apartments.

While Bunker Hill awaited these developments, the area immediately to the south of the Hill gradually became the city's new commercial core. Projects built since 1964 represented more than $1.1 billion worth of construction. Downtown was poised to become a regional focal point for business growth. In 1969 ARCO plaza was built at a cost of $190 million by Atlantic Richfield and Bank of America to house their national and southern California headquarters. It was the opinion of author John Weaver that razing the Art Deco black and gold Richfield building erased the ebullience of the 1920s. What ARCO has preserved is a scale model of that Morgan, Walls and Clements new Moderne design of 1928.

In accordance with the CRA plan, and with City Council approval, demolition continued to level standing structures on Bunker Hill. Declared Cultural Historical Monument No. 27 in 1964, the stately old Donegan residence, known as the Castle, was one of the last homes still rooted to Bunker Hill. Donegan's old coach house at 323 South Bunker Hill Avenue was considered a hazard and had already been demolished.

A smaller "salt box" style home, built in 1880 at 339 South Bunker Hill Avenue, received historical monument status on August 6, 1962. As Cultural Heritage Monument No. 5, just behind the Angels Flight historic designation, it was slated to be moved along with the Castle. However, it was years after the designation of Los Angeles Cultural Historical status that the large frame structure and the salt box home

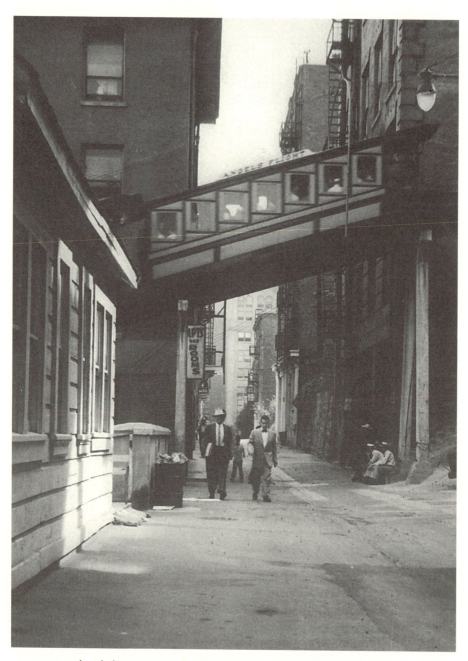

Angels Flight passes over Clay Street, more an alley, in the 1950s.
Photo T. S. Hall, courtesy Huntington Library.

Angels Flight over Clay Street, 1969. Photo courtesy Julius Shulman.

were successfully transported to the site of a planned historical park. Located at 3800 Homer Street, across the Arroyo Seco flood control channel, paralleling the Pasadena Freeway, the site was in Highland Park, a suburb just a few miles from the Civic Center. Currently operated by the Cultural Heritage Foundation and dedicated to the architectural re-creation of the Victorian era in Los Angeles, the site is known as Heritage Square.

On March 6, 1969, two months before Angels Flight was dismantled, the smaller "salt box" house and the Donegan mansion, which was cut in two sections to ease the move, were brought to the ten-acre site. By the next morning the Donegan Castle, along with the salt box house, no longer existed. They had been burned to the ground by vandals. The smoky ash of those venerable wood structures represented the last vestige of the golden era of old Bunker Hill.

In the early months of 1969 plans were made to discuss Angels Flight week. There would be a proclamation by the Mayor, and both Las Angelitas del Pueblo and the Beverly Hills Parlor, No. 289 of the Native Daughters of the Golden West would be asked to participate in a planned ceremony. At that time the CRA was requested to make a detailed photographic record prior and during the dismantling of Angels Flight in order to assure the proper replacement of the historic railway.

A notice, titled "Angels Flight," had been posted by the CRA on the site of the railway and read: "Angels Flight will temporarily discontinue service as of 10:30 p.m., Sunday, May 18, 1969. Angels Flight will be disassembled and stored until the time when the top of Bunker Hill has been graded. It is hoped that this will take no longer than two years. Then Angels Flight will be reassembled in the same location. To mark the temporary closing, there will be a brief ceremony, Friday, May 16, at 12:30 p.m. All passengers may ride free the last weekend. Schedule of free rides. Friday, May 16 - 1:00 p.m. to 10:30 p.m.; Saturday, May 17 and Sunday May 18 - 7:00 a.m. to 10:30 p.m."

On the weekend of May 16 - 18, 1969, for the last time until restoration, the 68 year-old incline railway would send the Olivet and Sinai counter-balancing up and down, past the demolition of old Bunker Hill. At the upper terminus of Angels Flight on Friday May 16, 1969 at 12:30 P.M. a ceremony referred to as "Pulling the Golden Spike," was sponsored by

Verdant trees lend a false sense of permanence to Angels Flight in this May 1969 photo by Julius Shulman.

Bunker Hill's Ems Hotel seen through the archway of Angels Flight in May of 1969. Photo courtesy Julius Shulman.

End of the line after dismantling of Angels Flight.
September 1969 photo, courtesy Eddy family collection.

Cultural Heritage Division of the Municipal Arts Department and the Community Redevelopment Agency. The ceremony was to "mark the closing of Angels Flight for approximately two years while the top of Bunker Hill is graded and improvements are made for further developments."

On the Sunday before the Flight's final ride, the Olivet and the Sinai carried approximately 3,100 paying customers. On the Flight's last memorable weekend, rides were free and around 40,000 passengers came for the last hurrah of Angels Flight. Members of the Electric Railway Historical Association of Southern California took the last ride on the Flight before it was "temporarily" closed. In the ERHA's newsletter, *Timepoints*, June 1969, it was reported that shortly after 10:30 p.m. when the last of the public had left the cars, members of ERHA boarded the Olivet. A near crush-load of members and their guests were on board for the Flight's last round trip, which began at 10:48 p.m. "Black flags were unfurled and the car descended to the bottom. David Cameron, former president of the Association, recalls watching the final closing down of the railway that evening at 10:53 p.m.

By May 19th it was all over. Dismantling began shortly thereafter with the archway and station house moved and relocated by Almas International to a Gardena salvage yard. At a cost of $225 a month the salient artifacts would stand exposed to the elements for over two decades. For a time the cable cars were stored in a warehouse at 1119 West 25th Street, operated by the Agency Rehousing, Property Management and Maintenance Department where the rental for sheltering the Olivet and Sinai was $150 a month.

Although Angels Flight had been dismantled, removed and stored for over a quarter of a century, former Bunker Hill Principal Planner Kawaratani has said that the Agency always planned to re-install the little railway and make it an integral part of the Hill's development in which Angels Flight would again become a major pedestrian circulation element for traversing the steep eastern slope of Bunker Hill. The retired CRA official shares the sentiment of Los Angeles citizenry that Angels Flight was a vital and loved historical icon of Downtown Los Angeles and had to be restored.

Even before the fabled incline railway made its last run in the spring of 1969, old Bunker Hill no longer existed. This sequestered hillsite, its amorphous 136 acres in the heart of a major city, was an anomaly. Many of its steep streets, first paved in 1903, followed a path of easiest access. Vegetation on the hill, represented by bright floral blooms, verdant trees, colorful winter weeds, had softened time's blows to the aging residential area, which had passed through some of the richest and starkest epochs in the history of Downtown Los Angeles. The end was devastating, leaving no vestige of what had been an eclectic collection of Victorian homes from an historic era.

English painter and writer John Ruskin, author of *The Seven Lamps of Architecture* (1849), wrote, "We may be able to live without architecture . . . but we cannot remember without her."

*A long-necked crane takes another chunk out of Bunker Hill whose regraded
vista allows a clear view of City Hall. 1957 photo T. S. Hall,
courtesy Huntington Library.*

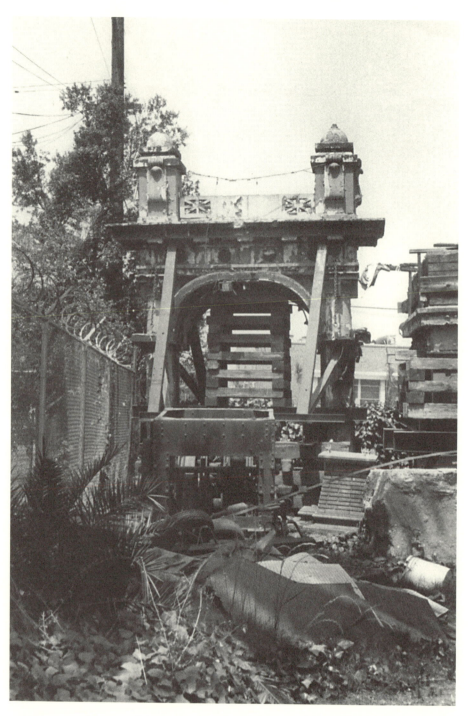

Historic archway and fountain-plaque in salvage yard storage prior to removal for restoration. Courtesy Graphic Arts, CRA.

Chapter Nine

Restoration

I n the summer of 1988 a reader of Jack Smith's column in the Los
Angeles *Times* asked the recurring question, "What happened to
Angels Flight?" In his inimitable fashion Mr. Smith succinctly replied,
"Angels Flight is crumbling away in some warehouse."

There was more than an element of truth in that commentary.
The retired cable cars were in storage, their designed tilt looking awkward
off their natural base of steep tracks. Yet concerned voices had never
stopped asking about the fate of Angels Flight. The Cultural Affairs
Commission, Los Angeles Conservancy, Cultural Heritage Foundation of
Southern California, Downtown Open Space Task Force, historical soci-
eties, citizens groups and general public fans of the funicular continued to
remind the Community Redevelopment Agency of its commitment to the
eventual restoration of Angels Flight.

Meanwhile, there was no dearth of ideas on how to proceed
with the preservation of the city's landmark railway. One suggestion would
have raised funds through the sale of souvenirs to be made from old
Angels Flight rails and spikes. Another suggestion was to rebuild the
funicular at Barnsdall Park to ease the climb for senior citizens who attended
the annual Garden Theater Festival. Knotts Berry Farm and Griffith Park
were also touted as possible locations for the Olivet and Sinai.

In the early spring of 1976 the CRA took a step toward restoring
Angels Flight by awarding a contract to R. Duell & Associates of
Santa Monica to study alternative locations, alignments, define code
requirements to rebuild and operate the little incline railway and help
prepare concepts to integrate it into Bunker Hill's new high-rise
development. It was generally accepted by the CRA that most of the
old equipment and the two small cars would have to be rebuilt.

In the winter of 1978 the Board of the Cultural Heritage
Commission spoke with representatives of Habbeger Industries, who had
made a presentation to the Community Redevelopment Agency regarding
a proposal to restore and re-install Angels Flight on Bunker Hill. The cars
had been inspected and pronounced capable of being restored. Because of
the change in the contour of the hill, it was estimated that some adjustment
would be have to be made for the difference in grade.

That same year the CRA asked the Cultural Heritage Foundation, which operates Heritage Square Museum, for assistance in preserving a portion of Angels Flight equipment at the Museum. The Agency had suggested that one of the cars might be placed in an interpretive exhibit on a steep bluff at the eastern edge of the Museum. The Foundation expressed the belief that it would be more appropriate to maintain the Angels Flight equipment intact and to exhibit it at one site as an operating exhibit rather than break it up among several locations for static display.

In an effort to save the Flight, the Foundation began negotiations which lasted a full year, granting the CRA permission to move all of the structures to the Museum for temporary storage in the Museum's materials yard. A plan was devised for one car, the Flight's archway and the drinking fountain with its memorial plaque to be placed at the Park. Soil testing, surveying and working drawings were prepared for a static exhibit. However, no action was taken and no part of Angels Flight ever came to Heritage Square.

The idea of putting one of the restored cars at Highland Park's Heritage Square and another in a museum setting at California Plaza was noted by Rodney Punt, Assistant General Manager of the Cultural Affairs Department. At a meeting with the CRA, Punt expressed a preference that "both historic cars be kept together rather than split between two locations." Keeping the Olivet and Sinai together was the favored option for the majority of followers of the funicular.

The CRA signed an agreement on February 5, 1982 for the development of the mixed-use $1.2 billion California Plaza project, which stipulated that Angels Flight be included as part of the project. By the end of 1983 the CRA would reiterate that the reinstallation of Angels Flight was linked to the commencement of construction of Phase 3A of California Plaza which was expected to occur around 1994. The agreement further stipulated that the developer would provide the setting, landscaping, walkways, etc. and was required to operate, maintain and preserve Angels Flight.

The Community Redevelopment Agency stated in May of 1983 that the Flight's two cars were in a condition of disrepair and could not possibly pass building code. The plans were to use 15% of the original

Olivet and Sinai in storage. Courtesy Graphic Arts, CRA.

materials from the cars in replicating Angels Flight. The length of the run would be shortened from 315 to 290 feet. Objections, articulated by David Cameron of the Los Angeles Conservancy, were made to this plan which was not implemented.

In 1989 the CRA approved design drawings for the Central Performance Plaza at California Plaza to locate the Angels Flight station house on its upper level. This location would provide for the Flight's original 33 percent track grade and allow use of the historic cars.

The Cultural Heritage Commission of the Department of Cultural Affairs had written a letter in September 1989 to the Community Redevelopment Agency stating that the Commission was "joined by other citizen groups in calling on the CRA to fulfill its promise made when Angel's Flight was removed from Bunker Hill, and finish the project which has lingered too long."

Part of the lingering too long had to do with the time taken to redevelop a major portion of Bunker Hill. It was nearly a decade after the dismantling of the Flight before the area had high-rise office buildings. In the late 1980s delays could be attributed to a depressed real estate market and poor economic conditions. This combination together with an earlier frenzy of office building in the Downtown area, made plans for California Plaza Three, to which the return of Angels Flight was tied, untenable.

By 1990 it was apparent that the next phase of development on California Plaza, the link to restoring Angels Flight, would be on indefinite hold. As Treasurer and a member of the Board of CRA Commissioners from 1990 to 1994, attorney Dennis R. Luna was an interested party to the proceedings of the return of Angels Flight. On December 18 of that year, Commissioner Luna made a motion designed to expedite the installation of Angels Flight. The motion would amend the work plan and in essence initiate a feasibility study of costs involved in beginning restoration immediately.

A Community Redevelopment Agency memorandum, dated September 19, 1991, made reference to a completed Angles Flight Historic Structures Report on the existing conditions of the station house and arch. Restoration architect, William Ellinger, found that while all the elements displayed "evidence of deferred maintenance . . . most of the historic fabric remains in essentially sound condition." Ellinger stated that for $3 million dollars the funicular could be built using the old cars, which would require variances of certain codes. An additional $900,000 would have to be spent to build it immediately.

Less than two weeks later Commissioner Luna suggested the creation of the Angels Flight Coordinating Committee. The object of the Committee was to oversee plans for the restoration and re-installation of the railway. A CRA memo was sent to the newly formed Committee concerning the "design parameters of the Angels Flight Restoration Workshop site plan." The site reference was on the northwest corner of Fourth and Hill streets. Members of the Committee, Chaired by Luna and numbering eight initially, represented a broad spectrum of citizens from Downtown's civic and business ranks, local preservation and conservation groups and residents of South Central Los Angeles.

Historic archway in support cribbing at Hill St. restoration site, 1995. Photo courtesy Harris & Associates.

The diversity of the members insured a wide range of interest and support for the funicular's return. By the time the Committee's mission was accomplished, there were twelve members, six of them from the original group.

The CRA had received a notice of lease termination on May 31, 1991 from the Underwriters Salvage of the Gardena salvage yard where the Angels Flight station house, arch and other historic artifacts had been stored since the spring of 1969. The notice was effective September 30, 1991, and Almas International, which had moved the Angels Flight items in 1969 from its original site, was selected to handle the move, which took place on October 31st. Between midnight and dawn on Halloween the station house and archway were quietly relocated to the CRA property, designated as the Angels Flight Restoration Workshop, at Fourth and Hill streets. Like ghostly figures on an old movie set, the weather-worn, decrepit relics of an era of old Bunker Hill remained until spring of 1995 waiting for restoration.

A few months after the relocation of the historic artifacts, the CRA Commission approved a contract with the Los Angeles Conservancy to establish and operate a restoration workshop program. Working behind the scenes with all the involved groups and organizations was the CRA's Bunker Hill Project Manager, Jeffrey Skorneck, who is credited with having been the Agency's energizing force in the restoration and return of Angels Flight.

In February of that year a second feasibility study developed a more specific plan to restore the incline railway. On August 19, 1992, the City Council authorized the CRA to enter into a contract with California Plaza, whereby California Plaza would restore and reconstruct Angels Flight. The following month Los Angeles County Transportation Commission, now the Metropolitan Transit Authority, approved $785,000 towards the reconstruction of the famed funicular.

In February 1992 an Angels Flight Re-Installation Refinement Study was submitted to the CRA by Parsons Brinckerhoff Quade and Douglas, Inc. Their findings reiterated that it was "technically and financially feasible to rehabilitate the original cars and buildings and put them into service."

Olivet on March 15, 1995 before restoration.
Courtesy Pueblo Contracting Services.

Harris & Associates, professional construction managers with headquarters in Concord, California, had been asked by the CRA late in 1991
to assist the Agency in developing a final design for the relocation and
restoration of Angels Flight. The CRA and Harris & Associates had
worked together in the past and by 1992 the Concord firm was involved
with plans and specifications for the restoration of the Flight as well as
codes and laws effecting its design and operation. The CRA and Harris &
Associates entered into an agreement in January of 1993 to serve as project
management consultant for Angels Flight restoration.

The City Council, on February 27, 1993, authorized the CRA
contract with Harris & Associates in which Harris & Associates would be
the project manager for the restoration and reconstruction of Angels
Flight. In the spring of that year the City Council approved a memorandum of understanding with the MTA whereby the MTA would fund

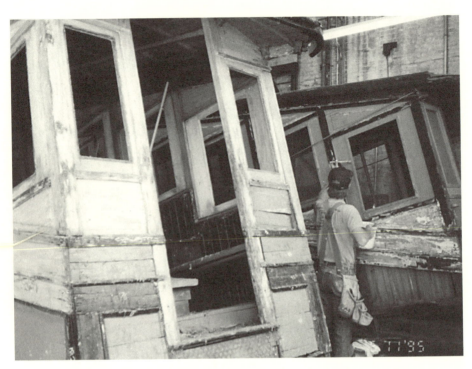

*Cars being stripped of layers of old paint. Photo spring of 1995,
courtesy Harris & Associates.*

$785,000 of the cost to reconstruct Angels Flight. Credited with helping
to make that happen was MTA alternate board member Nick Patsaouras,
for whom the new MTA headquarters has been named. A month later
the Cultural Heritage Commission approved the restoration and reconstruction plan for the city icon. The following day, June 17, 1993, the
CRA requested the Los Angeles City Council to approve an 18-month
restoration and reconstructive plan for the fabled Flight. A month later
approval was given by the City Council. From the last quarter of 1993
to the first quarter of 1994 detailed design drawings were prepared to bid
packages. Award contracts were issued by the CRA through 1994.

On Thursday March 9, 1995, after a month of rain, the sun
glinted on six brass trumpets poised to sound a fanfare, heralding the
ground-breaking ceremonies for Angels Flight. Gathering at Fourth and
Hill streets, just one-half block from the historic funicular's original site,

*Trumpeters herald the ground-breaking ceremony March 9, 1995.
Photo Bill Hunter. Author's collection.*

Pieces of cleaned signage on the historic archway at Pueblo Construction site. Photo V. L. Comer, summer 1995.

were delegates of the City of Los Angeles, the Community Redevelopment Agency, Cultural Affairs Commission, and the Citizens Downtown Open Space Task Force. Joining the dignitaries were representatives of Harris & Associates, Historic Resources Group, Pueblo Contracting Services, Tetra Design, California Plaza, the Los Angeles Conservancy, Metropolitan Transit Authority, Grand Central Market and The Yellin Company, the Angelus Plaza Resident Council, senior citizens from Angelus Plaza and a group of students from a local high school and elementary school. All representatives were sponsors or co-sponsors of the event. On display for the ceremony was the Olivet, a nostalgic reminder of the role of the funicular for residents and tourists on old Bunker Hill.

Members of the Moreland family, last private owners of Angels Flight, were part of the audience which crowded under the tented area or stood in the open spaces on the workshop site. Historical society members from Los Angeles County, heartened to see the first tangible evidence of the return of the beloved funicular, came to witness what the CRA termed, "A promise made, a promise kept."

With offices in Hollywood, the Historic Resources Group, directed the process of restoration, beginning in the spring of 1995, when the venerable cars were brought to 1313 West Sixth Street in Downtown Los Angeles. HRG had been an integral team member of the Flight's restoration project and prepared an historic structures report which included a history of the monument's construction, descriptive and photographic documentation as well as a description of existing conditions of the Angels Flight elements prior to rehabilitation with recommendations for its restoration. HRG monitored the project on site to protect historic elements of the station structures and rail cars, assure conformity with approved construction drawings and the appropriateness of new elements required for code compliance and railway operation.

Concerning an examination of the exterior of the Olivet, restoration architect Martin Weil reported that the original wood features were painted with a cream color oil base paint and the exterior wood elements were painted as many as sixteen times. Weil found that the first four finishes were monochromatic with subsequent coats of paint on the body of the car a bright orange except for one finish which was apricot. The trim was black. Weil's examination of the interior of the Olivet revealed that all the wood was either varnished or shellacked throughout most of its use. There were only four or five coats of orange or black paint over the varnish or shellac. His recommendation was that all sound paint layers be preserved as physical evidence of the evolution of Angels Flight and for conservation in the future.

During the early stages of restoration at the Sixth Street warehouse, deterioration of the Olivet and the Sinai was immediately obvious. Paint on the car bodies was cracked, scuffed, peeling; small sections of wood were broken off here and there. Architectural preservation consultant, Larry Winans, admitted that in addition to wood rot and age-deterioration, there was more hidden damage in the car frames. Winans described the construction of the cars as having an ordinary canvas roof, Douglas Fir with a sheathing of mahogany, paneling of white pine with pine exterior. The flooring was maple and original slats on the passenger

Finish carpenter Bruce Hartman restores a section of the old Station House at the Pueblo Construction site, summer 1995. Courtesy Pueblo Contracting Services.

seats were mahogany. Carefully stripping away layers of paint from the dry and faded surfaces revealed varying shades of orange, a panel of medium green with black trim and a bottom layer of a cream color. One cream-colored panel was decorated with a scroll, dating the paint to the turn of the century.

In the San Fernando Valley, Pueblo Contracting Services, the project's prime contractor, had the task of preparing the twenty-ton Hill Street archway, the station house and other pertinent artifacts of the Flight for final restoration. Overseeing that phase of restoration and reconstruction was the job of Martha Diaz Aszkenazy, president of the company. She acknowledged the challenge of balancing the historical aspect with the need to conform to current building codes. The railway structure had to be seismically sound while also retaining 60 percent of the original material to preserve the funicular's status as a cultural historic landmark. Specifically, slices of the original cement archway were applied as veneer to a new concrete frame.

With more than 200 dismantled pieces of the railway, each piece, each cornice and corbel, along with all the components of the entrance arch, the concrete and redwood station house, were numbered and cataloged by art conservator, Carolyn Lehne, with the assistance of Doug Cottone, Pueblo's project engineer whose task involved keeping track of all details and elements of the precast restoration.

Conservator Lehne, of KC Restoration in Malibu, found a variety of artifacts in the dismantling of the station house. Long folded sections of the Los Angeles *Record*, dated June 4, 1910, and uniformly folded short sections of the Los Angeles *Express* with a June 21, 1910 date were wedged in the concrete. A green matchbook with green tipped matches advertised " Girls Galore" at the Cottage, 215 1/2 West Fourth Street. There were business cards, a handbook dated 1920 titled, "Watch Your English" and a checkbook from the Third and Olive Branch of the Hellman Bank.

The Pueblo crew, mindful of the history and beauty of the cleaned artifacts and the one-of-a-kind experience the restoration presented, gave meticulous attention to details of their handiwork. Woodworking aspects of the restoration were headed by finish carpenter Bruce Hartman of Pagoda Construction, who was in charge of dismantling the archway, station house and artifacts. His knowledge of construction detail was utilized in the dismantling process in order to assure precision in re-assembling. For that reason Hartman also assisted cataloguer Carolyn Lehne in listing each and every piece of the venerable Flight's artifacts.

Hartman found interesting details which surfaced under layers of paint, such as the hand-etched redwood scrolls. Working with the wooden station house was another of the delicate restoration tasks assigned to Hartman. Under his direction, the cleaning and restoring of the single wall structure, the windows and doors brought back the luster of their fine redwood paneling. Flooring in the station house was the same hard maple as the flooring on the Olivet and Sinai. Hartman noted another restoration aspect of the station house: an operator's bathroom, measuring 2' x 6,' which had an old-fashioned flush box, activated by a pull chain.

Angels Flight station house during early stage of restoration on site, summer 1995. Courtesy Harris & Associates.

Donald Kahn, Pueblo's Project Manager, was in charge of the design-build aspect and responsible for putting the restoration process on paper in the form of plans. Kahn, representing Pueblo at team meetings, kept the time line on all Flight projects. Working with Kahn was David Johnson, structural engineer of David D. B. Johnson, Structural Engineers, responsible for tracks and trestles.

Civil Engineer Jerry Gross of the CRA, explained that extensive research had been done in terms of what had been originally built and it was obvious that much of the work had been done by craftsmen. According to Gross, if the restoration hit a snag, reference could be made to the original plans.

Professional Engineer James Guerrero, managing the construction phase of the project, guided the progress as over 60 sheets of plans and 450 pages of specifications were turned into a restored Flight. With his temporary office in the Bradbury Building and the work site of Angels Flight on Bunker Hill, Guerrero was retracing steps from the turn of the century in the Historic Core, going from the National Historic Landmark, Bradbury Building, to the Historic Cultural Landmark, Angels Flight.

Just after the March ground-breaking ceremony, drilling of the cassions, which form the column support, began at the project's Olive Street site. All restoration at the work site was under the supervision of Brian Leahey, Pueblo's Project Superintendent. Concrete was poured for the support columns and podium which houses the drive system for the railway. When the top of the podium was completed in May, it became the setting for the historic columns of the station house whose original trusses of Douglas Fir with redwood siding had been set in place supporting the original ceiling boards.

While at the workshop site on Hill Street, the station house and columns had been dry scraped of lead-based paint. Returned from the Pueblo site and raised to their permanent setting, detailed restoration was completed on the podium. The 9,000 pound sheave, cleaned and gleaming black, was set in the station house where it remains as an exhibit artifact. The sheave is a large wheel with a grooved rim, mounted in a pulley block to guide the cable.

To allow for the insertion of steel reinforcing rods to meet earth-quake standards, precast concrete sections of the arches had to be cut.

Putting the puzzle pieces together often required cranes to lift the ponderously heavy precast concrete artifacts. In mid-October a 175 ton off-shore crane, with a boom length of 160 feet, was used to set the precast concrete railway ties in place. The Krup Model crane, one of the biggest in California, came down from Ventura via Offshore Crane and Service Company.

Tetra Design, headed by native Angeleno Robert Uyeda, F.A.I.A., was selected as the Architect-of-Record for Angels Flight. The Los Angeles firm, with Gene Directo, architect, as Tetra's Angels Flight Project Manager, was responsible for the design of the Olive Street podium as well as overseeing restoration of the cars, arch, and station house.

In the process of structurally stabilizing the archway, it was discovered that the old steel columns, encased in concrete, and the concrete beam between the arch columns had deteriorated due to water penetration. A new cast-in-place concrete beam with the signage, balustrade, keystones and scrolls had to be reset and pinned.

Most of the original fabric, according to Tetra, was used for the station house with the exception of the pavilion which has been constructed of reinforced concrete spandrel beams and columns. The column capitals and base plinths, however, were cored and reused as were the original redwood pavilion ceiling boards. Existing roof sheathing of the station house has been supplemented with new anchorage and a new shear wall on the south side with the existing siding as exterior finish and new wood siding to match inside. In order to obtain a modification from the Fire Department to allow a wood structure to be constructed in a non-combustible zone, the station house is fully sprinklered and coated in fire retardant paint.

Tetra's design team discovered that the passenger cars Olivet and Sinai had sustained damage to their historic fabric in the process of moving the cars from one warehouse location to another. Those damaged portions, together with sections of the wood undercarriage and vertical ribs which exhibited dry rot, were replaced and new wood shear panels were installed to tie the car structure together. To supplement each car chassis an inverted steel tee beam was inserted and attached to the wood framing. For the first time the historic cars have steel undercarriages.

Modification of the historic fabric of one car to provide wheelchair access was made even though a special rule of the 1990 Americans With

Another stage of restoration before removal of the car seats, summer 1995.
Courtesy Harris & Associates.

Construction at the Olive Street Bridge with station house on top, August 1995.
Courtesy Pueblo Contracting Services.

Disabilities Act (ADA) would have exempted Angels Flight. The special rule pertains to "historical or antiquated rail passenger cars." Specifically, the modification involved removal of one seat in the upper, open end of the Sinai, the car on the north side of the run, and alteration of the car's historic grille. This modification allowed the wrought-iron grille to function as a door to admit the wheelchair. At the bottom of the Flight, on the north side of the Hill Street Archway, a gate has been installed for wheelchair access. When a button by the gate is pushed, it signals the operator at the terminus to release the gate's lock. Inside a short stairway contains an inclined lift to carry the wheelchair onto the Sinai's upper end.

Original cable equipment, used to operate the cars, will be on display but not operational. Extensive coordination between the design and design-build teams combined to ensure that the operating systems for the funicular provided a balance to retain both the historic fabric and a safe, smooth performance of the railway. According to Zyg Kunczynski, Project Engineer for Yantrak, the Carson City firm responsible for the railway's system, "Each vehicle is pulled up the track by a cable which is stored on a drum 72" in diameter. The system is powered by one Sterling Electric 100 horsepower motor and operates at 5.9 feet per second. The funicular is automatically controlled by a fiber optic link system, pre-programmed by Yantrak. That system is linked to a desktop computer which provides a user interface for the operator."

A striking contrast exists between the space-cramped station house with its historical artifacts and the open, airy room with cabinets of computer wiring and switches on the second level of the podium. There two massive spool drums dominate one corner of the nerve center of the Flight's operating system. Yantrak's electrician, Carl Stewart, points out that the track has been equipped with proximity switches, which sense the location of the vehicles and communicate to the computer. As a vehicle approaches the terminal, the computer gradually reduces motor speed until the vehicle has docked. As a safety feature there are also independent switches that sense car position and will cause the system to stop if any abnormality occurs.

Yantrak custom designed and installed the operating system which includes twin Caterpillar D-9 gear assemblies between the two huge drums, which are grooved to accommodate the cable and prevent wear from slippage. Stewart noted that having a separate cable for each car adds years of life to the cable. He emphasized that the Flight is no less a funicular for having the two cables and points out that the Flight, like a modern elevator, is controlled by a Programmable Logic Controller (PLC). When the start switch is activated in the station house, a deafening sound announces the rolling of the black drums, coiling and uncoiling cable as the cars move upward and downward on the track. There is an emergency brake as well as a brake for each of the powerful drums.

Along the southern edge of the track and trestle an emergency stairway, recalling the original pedestrian stairway required by the City in 1901, was constructed just beyond the Hill Street entrance. The concrete stairway leading up to the Olive Street level has 117 steps, measuring 12 1/2" across with 6" risers. Between the uneven series of steps, there are half a dozen flat walking areas of varying length. At the end of the concrete steps, a steel stairway offers access to the 370 foot level of the podium.

Exterior podium structure design had to be sensitive to the modern statement of the high-rise office building known as California Plaza Two and the historic statement of the Angels Flight station house while maintaining the separate and distinct identities of each. Until a Phase Three is developed, the southeastern edge of the podium will be visually prominent. To that end, Tetra designed the podium to allow the southern portion to be demolished at a later date making way for California Plaza Three.

Landscaping for Angels Flight was coordinated with "Angels Walk," a pedestrian network linking the Historic Downtown Core with the new subway stations. On the south side of the archway, a new walk and plaza provide space for queueing as well as to watch the Olivet and the Sinai as they carry passengers up and down the hill. This broad sidewalk with insets of fourteen young eucalyptus trees becomes part of the "Angels Walk," designed to provide safe, pleasant and convenient access to the Metro Rail Network. Representing an effort to revitalize segments of Downtown Los Angeles, the walkway connects the lower entrance of Angels Flight with the Metro Red Line portal at the northwest corner of Fourth and Hill streets, thereby linking the restored Flight to part of the network of the City's transportation infrastructure.

Close-up of the Beaux Arts station house with a California Plaza tower in the background. 1996 photo courtesy Doug Piburn.

Over-view of restructured Bunker Hill and restored Angels Flight.
Photo Erhard Pfeiffer. Courtesy California Plaza.

Chapter Ten

Return to Bunker Hill

Even before the little funicular had made its last run in 1969, assurances were given that Angels Flight would be returned soon. "Yes, Virginia, there will still be an Angel's Flight," wrote Gilbert W. Lindsay, former Ninth District Councilman, in a column dated May 13, 1969, just three days before the final rides. Two was the magic number. Lindsay stated it would be "in storage . . . for about two years." Less than two weeks after the dismantling, Carl S. Dentzel, president of the Cultural Heritage Board noted that, "it was gratifying to this Board to be able to pass on to interested citizens the Community Redevelopment Agency's assurance that Angel's Flight would be restored to service within approximately two years."

Some fourteen years later an editorial in the Los Angeles *Times*, September 7, 1983, "The Long, Long Wait," counted on CRA assurances that "one of Los Angeles' most famous landmarks will be in service by 1988." The article concluded, "Nineteen years is a long time to wait for the next train to come along." Angelenos continued to wait. In 1979 the Los Angeles *Times* ran a Dick Turpin column entitled "Renewed Angel's Flight Integral Element in Bunker Hill Program." The article quoted then Mayor Tom Bradley, "Angel's Flight, like the phoenix, will rise again and an historic chapter of Los Angeles' past will once again be a reality. And unlike many other cultural monuments, Angel's Flight will be functional, not just something to look at and admire, but something to use."

John Benzing, Deputy Director of Engineering for the City's Redevelopment Agency, who started as the Angels Flight Project Engineer in 1985, was the CRA's representative on the Flight's restoration team. Benzing expressed the common thread running through the entire project, a realization of the historical import of Los Angeles' little incline railway and the need for its return to Bunker Hill.

On November 30th, Pueblo Contracting Services hosted a traditional "Topping Out" party to celebrate the team-work of everyone involved with the near-completion of the restoration and installation of Angels Flight. Speaking briefly were representatives of the offices of the Mayor and Councilwoman of the Ninth District, Historic Resources Group, the CRA and Keller Construction, joint-venture partners with

Pueblo. Awards of recognition were made by Sev Aszkenazy, vice-president of Pueblo Contracting. The conclusion of the "Topping Out" was the dramatic unveiling of the Olivet, which had been trucked over from its restoration location for the ceremony. Freshly painted and nearly ready for service, the Olivet spent a brief time on display before being returned to the warehouse for more finishing touches.

By the end of December the project's team of professionals worked on completing restoration of the ornate station house and entrance arch on Hill Street. Meanwhile, volunteers, including the author and Alma Carlisle, former city preservationist, worked at the Pasadena "Rose Palace" on the Angels Flight float for the New Year's Day Rose Parade. With pride and nostalgia the City of Los Angeles sponsored the Angels Flight entry in the 107th Rose Parade. In brilliant January sunshine the fifty-five foot float, with its chrysanthemum-covered cable car and entrance arch, rolled down Pasadena's Colorado Boulevard.

Like the entry in the Rose Parade, Bunker Hill's Angels Flight had been painted orange with black trim the last week of December. Earlier, stripped of the layers of old paint, sections of the ornate arches and columns were temporarily returned to the white concrete structure designed by Train and Williams in 1910.

By the end of January, the railway's straight track had been installed and the curved track was in place. On a grey Tuesday morning a construction crane hoisted the historic little cars onto the tracks. First the Sinai was set down by the archway and a few hours later the Olivet was lifted onto the tracks close to the upper terminus station house. During February the drive system, which includes the cable, sheaves and electronic controls, was tested. Hill Street pedestrians often stopped to watch the quaint cable cars moving slowly up and down their runs while the load weight of the two cars was being monitored. A curious observer, looking into the cars during the load testing, might have seen the seating bays occupied by plastic covered cases of beverage. Though the test requirement weight was 8,700 pounds, the test load weight was 9,000 pounds. With the successful completion of the engineering tests, the California Public Utilities Commission certified the operation of Angels Flight.

With the long wait finally over, passengers entering on Hill Street

The Olivet, heading down the steep incline, slips past the Sinai,
February 1996. Photo Deane Romano.

pass under the historic archway of the early 1900s to board Angels Flight, less than a block from its original site. The restored Olivet and Sinai run on new tracks to and from the original ornate station house, also meticulously restored. Instead of landing at Olive Street, the funicular now has its "head house" on a bridge over Olive. The formidable bridge with its 100 ton girders is 142 feet long and 12 feet high.

On the other side of the Olive Street bridge, Angels Flight makes a re-connection with what was historic Bunker Hill. California Plaza, the Flight's terminus, is described promotionally as a "Community where the worlds of finance, commerce, culture, entertainment and elegant residential accommodations form an innovative living mosaic in Downtown Los Angeles." Michael Alexander, Artistic Director of California Plaza Presents, expressed the Plaza's enthusiasm for the return of Angels Flight linking the new Bunker Hill with its Downtown past and offering an opportunity to residents and visitors who may not have experienced the performing arts series and the beauty of the Watercourt displays. Alexander believes that the beloved landmark will help travelers discover the center of Los Angeles and will re-introduce Downtown to its residents.

Riders of Angels Flight arrive at the upper level of California Plaza's Watercourt when they step off the funicular at the railway's station house. From that point visitors have an up-close look at the gleaming glass and glittering steel towers, the shops, the amenities, the colorful landscaping, the turn-of-a-new-century Bunker Hill. At the Watercourt level, California Plaza Presents offers free-to-the-public seasonal entertainment in a setting of water pyrotechnics which is a show in itself as a waterfall rushes over terraced steps to a small lake.

Overlooking the Watercourt, the Inter-Continental Hotel has kept a vestige of old Bunker Hill with conference rooms which bear historic names of the Hill's mansions. Widney, Bradbury, Rose, Hershey, Crocker and Brunson rooms display California artist Gerald Brommer's original pen and wash drawings of each Victorian mansion.

Facing Grand Avenue, a short walk from the Inter-Continental, the Museum of Contemporary Art is notable for the distinctive barrel-vault roof design of architect Arata Isozaki. Continuing on Grand, across First Street, the Music Center, initiated in 1964, anchors the north end of Bunker Hill. This project was the result of the Community Redevelopment

California Plaza's Watercourt. 1994 Photo by Bill Varie.
Courtesy California Plaza.

Lloyd Hamrol's "Uptown Rocker." Amy Stone photo.
Courtesy Author's Collection.

Agency's attempt to stimulate downtown Los Angeles'
revitalization by orchestrating a number of development plans over a
period of years. At that time, the trio of cultural centers, Ahmanson
Theatre, Mark Taper Forum and Dorothy Chandler Pavilion, made the
Hill's run-down housing an incongruous neighbor. Today the high-rise
apartments, offices and court buildings of the Music Center's environs
flesh out aspects of a burgeoning city.

On Hope Avenue a long stairway to Fifth Street represents a
showpiece of the restructuring of Bunker Hill. Designed by landscape
architect Lawrence Halprin, the wide, sweeping steps run in the corridor
between the tallest building on the West Coast, the 73-story First
Interstate World Center, and the back of the 444 South Flower Street
Building. Reminiscent of Rome's Spanish steps, a water runnel becomes
the center balustrade of the stairway which connects Bunker Hill with the
Los Angeles Public Library, handsomely renovated after a disastrous arson
fire in the spring of 1986.

On the regraded, recontoured, multi-level streets of modern Bunker Hill tall, sleek buildings shape steep canyons connected by open walkways of brick and granite, bordered by marble-sided planters with seasonal varieties of flowering plants. Developers' prerequisite public art is evident in a diversity of metal sculptures. The courtyard of Wells Fargo Plaza is the site of "Night Sail," a towering piece by the noted sculptress, Louise Nevelson. Looking down from the Grand Avenue level onto Fourth Street offers a view of Lloyd Hamrol's $135,000 "Uptown Rocker."

One block west of Grand Avenue is the area where Bunker Hill Avenue ran across the crest of the hill between Grand and Hope. The forty foot wide street had been home to Judge Julius Brousseau, D. F. Donegan's doomed castle and once a special neighborhood of families, friends and flowering vegetation. Like two-block long Clay Street, which ran under Angels Flight between Hill and Olive, and the block-long Cinnabar Street, paralleling Hope and Flower between Second and Third streets, there is no discernible sense of Bunker Hill Avenue's former place.

Nothing suggests a lost residential area with impressive mansions, lawns and tree-lined streets of another era. At the southeast corner of Grand and Fourth there is no evidence of the Leonard J. Rose residence, one of the Hill's most expensive Victorians, which once claimed approximately that space. No imprint remains of the later community of pensioners and other persons who lived in the aging Victorians, enjoying their unique environs in the heart of a major city.

Anyone looking for the original site of Angels Flight at Third and Olive streets would not be able to reconcile the area with old photographs. The turreted and imposing Crocker mansion at the top of the Flight had already been replaced in 1909 by the new temple of the Benevolent and Protective Order of Elks.

In the cavity left by the removal of Angels Flight in 1969, Angelus Plaza filled in all the blanks. Their first building was a seventeen-story apartment complex forming a community for senior adults. Referred to as "a vertical Leisure World on Hill Street," Angelus Plaza, a $58 million project, was the largest subsidized senior housing community in the nation. Today the seemingly unending structure of Angelus Plaza runs from a Hill Street parking garage to an apartment complex which crosses over the tunnel itself past Third to Second Street. The sprawling project of four high-rise buildings now covers much of the area which was once the two-block long Clay Street.

Approximately half a block from that original site, the official Re-Dedication of Angels Flight began at 9 a. m. on Friday February 23, 1996 under crystalline blue skies and bright sunshine. Mayor Richard J. Riordan, Ninth District Council Member Rita Walters, Community Redevelopment Agency Chair Christine Essel, Metropolitan Transportation Authority Chairman Larry Zarian and Angels Flight Railway Foundation Chairman Dennis R. Luna each spoke on behalf of the historic occasion.

A common thread of enthusiasm ran through the remarks of each speaker; a common awareness of the historic moment coupled with reminiscence of a youthful ride on the fabled Flight. Mayor Riordan expressed the pride of restoring "an important piece of our historical fabric," which is "truly a gift for our future generations." He defined Los Angeles as "a city with a glorious past . . . and an incredible future," and pledged to continue to support the preservation of Los Angeles' historic heritage.

Three Re-Dedication plaques, located on the south side of the track near the Hill Street entrance, were unveiled before the Mayor and Council Member Walters rode the ascending car along with a group of seniors and children. The descending car carried the Los Angeles Master Chorale singing "Funiculi, Funicula." Invited guests and the news media paid twenty-five cents each each way for preview test rides.

Included among the enthusiastic audience at the morning ceremony were heirs and descendants of former owners of Angels Flight. Sharing part of a unique legacy were Lester Moreland's family, Robert and Barbara Moreland, their daughter, son and grandchildren. Robert Mackay Moore, who had no offspring, was represented by his grand-nieces and grand-nephews, including Charles and Kay Richey, their children and grandchildren. Among descendants of Colonel James Ward Eddy, the original founder of Angels Flight, was the great, great grandson of Colonel Eddy, Jim Coughlin, who flew in from Arizona to join his sister, Gypsy Cherryholmes and other family members. Jim wore the Colonel's gold watch, inscribed with the initials *JWE*, which had been willed to his grandfather, Simeon Eddy Gillette.

All that sunny morning and afternoon, ceremony guests rode the

Mayor Riordan at the Re-Dedication Ceremony February 23, 1996.
Photo by Doug Piburn.

Olivet and Sinai from Hill Street to the station house at the Watercourt
level of California Plaza and back again. That evening, a fund-raising gala,
"First Night At Angels Flight," offered preview free rides on the restored
funicular for guests of the event. Organizers of the evening and recipients
of the proceeds were Angels Flight Railway Foundation, KCET Women's
Council and the Los Angeles Conservancy.

At 9:30 a.m. the following morning, with a repeat of clear blue
skies and brilliant sunshine, sounds of a marching band announced the
beginning of festivities for the Re-Opening event. At 10:00 a.m. the
Master of Ceremonies introduced Robert Moreland, who made a brief
address. Public recognition was made to all the families of previous Flight
owners as well as specific individuals for their support of Angels Flight in

The Sinai carries the first wheelchair passenger. Re-Dedication Ceremony, February 23, 1996. Photo by Doug Piburn.

the past and/or for their contribution to the restoration and return of Angels Flight. John Welborne, the Flight's manager-operator, was among those persons singled out for recognition along with the venerable artist and author, Leo Politi.

After the speeches and recognition, Angels Flight, Bunker Hill's beloved icon, was re-opened to the general public after a 27 year hiatus. It was after 10:30 a.m. when the first car left the Hill Street entrance for the opening ride. Among the passengers were "First Families" of Angels Flight, old Bunker Hill's resident artist Leo Politi and Electric Railway Historical Association member David Cameron.

Hundreds of spectators, motivated by nostalgia and excitement, lined up for a chance to be part of the historic moment. With a fare of twenty-five cents each way, ticket books (valid for one person only) offered five rides for $1.00 and 40 rides for $7.50. Eager passengers rode from the Hill Street entrance up to the Watercourt level of California Plaza where they were greeted with music and entertainment.

A street faire, running from 9 a.m. to 6 p.m. that weekend, on the Third to Fourth Street block of Hill, celebrated the Flight's opening. A variety of entertainment was offered at the Watercourt stage on the California Plaza level and the adjacent Angelus Plaza Senior Activity Center. Paintings of old Bunker Hill and Angels Flight were the focus of an art exhibit featuring the works of Ben Abril, Stanton Manolakas and Leo Politi. In a last public appearance, revered artist Politi was on hand to autograph prints of one of his paintings of the old Angels Flight

From Hill Street to Olive patrons of Angels Flight moved easily up the eastern slope of Bunker Hill, riding the restored Olivet or the Sinai, which slipped almost soundlessly over the tracks. Visitors to the Flight could exercise their option to ascend or descend on the south side of the railway via stairs. Wheelchair access to the Sinai on that ceremonious weekend was available via a portable chair lift on the north side of the Hill Street archway.

Typifying many of the delighted passengers who returned to experience a nostalgic moment on Angels Flight, Leonard Bernstein had remembered the Flight as not seeming to have a beginning or an end; it was a destination in itself. Like most of the riders, he felt the little railway was "a comfortable, pleasant memory, associated with family and good times." Bernstein brought his own children to the re-opening to continue the thread of pleasant associations with Angels Flight.

In addition to the warmth of its reception from riders of the Flight, there have been awards for the restoration of the incline railway. In April the Community Redevelopment Agency accepted an award for Downtown's "Best Renovation" and in May Angels Flight Railway was given the President's Award in the 1996 Preservation Awards by the Los Angeles Conservancy.

According to architectural historians, David Gebhard and Robert Winter, it was the realization of the substantial loss of Bunker Hill's Victorians which led to the founding of the Cultural Heritage Foundation in 1969. The late Dr. Gebhard had pointed out that, "Contrary to popular belief, organized preservation efforts have had a long history in Los Angeles. The California Landmarks Club, founded in 1894, under the leadership of

Angels Flight tickets from 1967 and the Re-Opening in 1996.
Author's collection.

February 24,1996. Angels Flight Re-Opening at the Olive Street Station House. Photo Doug Piburn.

Charles F. Lummis, pioneered conservation of historic architecture."

The Los Angeles Conservancy, since its inception in 1978, has had a close and watchful connection with Angels Flight. Conservancy Director Linda Dishman, was enthusiastic about the restoration and re-opening of the incline railway and expressed the hope that it might set a precedent for Los Angeles' historic preservation.

A restored Angels Flight bridges the chasm of Los Angeles' nostalgic past between those who remember the little railway and the role it played on Bunker Hill and those who never had ridden the celestial railway or known its historic background. In addition to the charm of nostalgia, the incline railway represents a connection between Bunker Hill, with its urbane, cosmopolitan activities, and the diverse character of the commercial neighborhoods on Hill Street and Broadway. Equally important are the related aspects of the fabled funicular and tourism. Angels Flight, as a symbol of Bunker Hill's illustrious past and its exhilarating future, will provide the magnet drawing visitors to Downtown. As a beloved landmark, it will once again become an icon, easily recognized as a unique exponent of the City of Los Angeles.

At the turn of another century a glittering Acropolis has emerged from the rubble of old Bunker Hill. Just over sixteen years after Mayor Bradley's emphatic promise, the mythical phoenix has risen from the ashes of Bunker Hill's urban renewal. Angels Flight is "not just something to look at and admire, but something to use." Like the fabled Arabian bird, Angels Flight is one of a kind and comes back to life to repeat the former one. This symbolic landmark, Angels Flight, returns to the downtown hill site as a powerful signature of the perseverance of its supporters.

Like a beacon the one-story station house with its Beaux Arts Revival architecture, stands distinctive in the foreground of towering structures of glass and steel. Angels Flight, an architectural anachronism, will serve to remind all who look at this symbol of the city's past that there is hope for conservancy and preservation of local history and its historical elements.

*Angels Flight, back on Bunker Hill, an architectural anachronism,
February 1996. Photo by Doug Piburn.*

CHRONOLOGY

1781	September 4 - Official establishment of Los Angeles as a pueblo
1786	*Pobladores* (settlers) given official title to pueblo lands
1835	Status of Los Angeles raised from *pueblo* (town) to *ciudad* (city)
1849	Lt. Edward O.C. Ord's survey of Los Angeles
1852	Arrival of Prudent Beaudry in Los Angeles
1867	Purchase by Beaudry of 20 acres of Bunker Hill at auction
1874	Debut of the Sixth & Spring Street Horse Car Line
1883	Southern Pacific Railroad opened to the East
1885	Opening of Second Street Cable Car, going up and over Bunker Hill
1893	July 4 - Opening of Mt. Lowe's Great Incline Railway, Rubio Canyon
1895	Arrival of Colonel and Isabella Eddy in Los Angeles
1901	Bunker Hill Tunnel completion; December 31, official opening of Angels Flight
1902	Establishment of Los Angeles Water Works, renamed Water Department.
1904	Opening of Court Flight at 208 North Broadway, between First and Temple
1905	First renovation of Angels Flight with enclosed cars and an elevated track.
1909	National Reunion of B. P. O. E. at new Lodge on 300 South Olive Street
1910	Second renovation of Angels Flight with landmark Beaux Arts Revival archway and station house, new cars and tracks

CHRONOLOGY

1911   Change in railway fare from 1 cent to 5 cents

1912   Sale of Angels Flight - Colonel J. W. Eddy to the Funding Company of CA

1913   First and last accident in history of Angels Flight

1914   Second sale of Angels Flight - Funding Company of California to Continental Securities, Robert M. Moore owner; repairs and reinforcement of railway and pavilion by Mercereau Bridge and Construction Company

1916   Death of Colonel J. W. Eddy in Eagle Rock, CA, April 12

1920s   Removal of 4 northern bays on original station house; replacement with pavilion

1929   Attempts by C. C. Bigelow (Southwest Investment Corporation) to remove Bunker Hill

1930s   Change to orange and black color scheme for Angels Flight

1934   Appearance of parking lots on former Bunker Hill residential sites

1935   Attempt by City Council to terminate the Railway's franchise

1938   Removal of Colonel Eddy's observation tower with camera obscura

1942   Shut-down of service of Court Flight 1st of October

1946   Transfer of Angels Flight title from Continental Securities to Robert M. Moore in liquidation of the company's assets

1948   Need for a Redevelopment Agency declared by City Council

CHRONOLOGY

1952   Retirement of R. M. Moore at age 85 and sale of Angels Flight to Byron Linville and Lester B. Moreland

1953   Death of Robert Mackay Moore in February. Retirement of Byron Linville and sale of his interest in Angels Flight to Lester B. Moreland on March 16; Increase in book fare from 50 rides for 50 cents to 30 rides for 50 cents

1958   Approval by U.S. Government of Bunker Hill Project

1959   Mandate by City Council for a Bunker Hill Urban Renewal Project

1961   Acquisition of Community Redevelopment Agency's first land on Bunker Hill

1962   Designation of Angels Flight as Cultural Historical Landmark No. 4 in August; Sale of Angels Flight to the Community Redevelopment Agency, October 16

1963   Reduction of Flight's operation: 7 a.m. to 10:30 p.m.

1965   First land sale of Bunker Hill, future site of the Union Bank Square

1969   Free rides, May 16 to May 18

1976   Contract awarded to R. Duell & Associates to study alternative locations and define aspects of the return of Angels Flight

1978   Formation of Los Angeles Conservancy

1981   Bicentennial celebration and selection of re-location site for Angels Flight

1982   Agreement by CRA for mixed-use development of California Plaza, including Angels Flight in the project

CHRONOLOGY

1991   Announcement or return of Angels Flight;
        Unveiling of Bicentennial Monument at
        California Plaza's Spiral Court (temporary
        location of monument). Creation of Angels
        Flight Coordinating Committee. Re-location
        of railway's station house and archway to
        corner of Fourth & Hill

1992   Contribution of $785,000 by Los Angeles
        County Transportation Commission
        (Metropolitan Transit Authority) for
        reconstruction and restoration of Angels Flight

1993   Harris and Associates authorized to serve as
        project management consultant for Angels Flight
        Project. Approval of $4 million for restoration
        and reconstruction of 18 month project

1994   Awarding of construction contract to Pueblo
        Contracting for reconstruction and restoration

1995   March 9th ground-breaking ceremony for
        Angels Flight

        Formation of the Angels Flight
        Railway Foundation

        Formation of Angels Flight Operating Company

        Topping Out ceremony by Pueblo Contracting
        Services

1996   January 1 Rose Parade entry of Angels Flight replica

        February 23 official Re-Dedication, February 24
        official Re-Opening of the Flight

SELECTED BIBLIOGRAPHY

Adler, Pat. *The Bunker Hill Story.* Glendale, CA, La Siesta Press, 1964

Bowman, Lynn, *Los Angeles; Epic of a City.* Los Angeles: Howell-North Books, 1974.

Carr, Harry. *Los Angeles: City of Dreams.* N.Y.: D. Appleton-Century Company, 1935.

Caughey, John and LaRee. *Los Angeles, Biography of a City.* Berkeley: University of California Press, 1976.

Chandler, Raymond. *The High Window.* New York: Alfred A. Knopf, 1942.

Cleland, Robert, Glass. *Cattle on a Thousand Hills. Southern California: 1850-1880*, San Marino, CA, Huntington Library, 1951.

Comer, Virginia L. *In Victorian Los Angeles: The Witmers of Crown Hill.* Los Angeles: Talbot Press, 1988.

Costello, Julia and Wilcoxson, Larry. *An Architectural Assessment of Cultural Resources in Urban Los Angeles.* Los Angeles: Bureau of Engineering, Department of Power and Water, 1979.

Cowan, Robert G. *On the Rails of Los Angeles: A Pictorial History of Its Street-cars.* Los Angeles: Historical Society of Southern California, 1971.

Crump, Spencer. *Ride The Big Red Cars.* Los Angeles: Crest Publications, 1962.

Dash, Norman. *Yesterday's Los Angeles.* Miami: E.A. Seemann Publishing, Inc., 1976.

Dumke, Glenn S. *The Boom of the Eighties in Southern California.* San Marino, CA: Huntington Library, 1944.

Gebhard, David and Robert Winter. *Architecture in Los Angeles: A Compleat Guide.* Salt Lake City, Peregrine Smith Books, 1985.

Graves, Jackson A. *My Seventy Years in California., 1857-1927.* Los Angeles; Times-Mirror Press, 1927.

Guinn, John Miller. *History of California and Los Angeles.* (Vol. 1 & 3), Los Angeles: Historic Record Company, 1915.

SELECTED BIBLIOGRAPHY

Hill, Laurance L. *La Reina Los Angeles in Three Centuries.*
Los Angeles: Security Trust and Savings, 1929.

Hylen, Arnold. *Bunker Hill, A Los Angeles Landmark.* Los
Angeles: Cultural Heritage Board of Los Angeles, 1976.

_____ . *Los Angeles Before the Freeways, 1850-1950.*
Los Angeles: Dawson's Book Shop, 1981.

_____ . *The Vanishing Face of Los Angeles.* Los Angeles:
Dawson's book Shop, 1968.

Kirker, Harold. *California's Architectural Frontier.* San Marino,
CA: Huntington Library, 1960.

Kuen, Gernot. *Views of Los Angeles.* Los Angeles: Portriga
Publications, 1978.

Mayer, Robert (Editor). *Los Angeles: A Chronological &
Documentary History.* Dobbs Ferry, NY: Oceana
Publications, 1978.

McGroarty, John Steven. *History of Los Angeles County.*
Chicago and New York: American Historical Society Inc.,
1923.

_____ . *Los Angeles From The Mountains To The Sea.*
Chicago and New York: The American Historical Society,
1921.

Nadeau, Remi. *City Makers: The Story of Southern California's
First Boom, 1868-1876.* Corona Del Mar, CA:
Trans-Anglo Books, 1977.

_____ . *Los Angeles: From Mission to Modern City.* New
York: Longmans, Green and Co., 1960.

Newmark, Harris. *Sixty Years in Southern California.* New
York: The Knickerbocker Press, 1916.

Newsom, Joseph Cather. *Artistic Buildings and Homes of Los
Angeles.* Los Angeles: Calliope Press, 1881.

Nordhoff, Charles. *California, For Health, Pleasure and
Residence.* New York: Harper & Brothers, 1872.

Nunis, Doyce B., Jr. (Editor). *Los Angeles and its Environs In
the Twentieth Century.* Los Angeles: The Ward Ritchie
Press, 1973.

SELECTED BIBLIOGRAPHY

O'Flaherty, Joseph S. *Those Powerful Years: The South Coast and Los Angeles, 1887-1917*. New York: Exposition Press, 1978.

Ord, Edward O. C. *The City of the Angels and the City of the Saints*. San Marino, CA: The Huntington Library, 1978.

Phillips, Mary Alice. *Los Angeles, A Guide Book*. Los Angeles: The Neuner Co., 1907.

Politi, Leo. *Bunker Hill, Los Angeles: Reminiscences of a Bygone Era*. Palm Desert, CA: Desert-Southwestern, Inc., 1964.

_____ . *Piccolo's Prank*. New York: Charles Scribner's Sons, 1965.

Powell, Lawrence Clark. *Land of Fiction*. Los Angeles, Dawson's Book Shop, 1952.

Robinson, W. W. *Los Angeles From The Days Of The Pueblo*. Los Angeles: California Historical Society, 1981.

_____ . *Maps of Los Angeles: From Ord's Survey to the End of the Boom of the Eighties*. Los Angeles: Dawson's Book Shop, 1966.

Rose, L. J., Jr. *L. J. Rose of Sunny Slope*. San Marino, CA: Huntington Library, 1959.

Ryan, Don. *Angel's Flight*. New York: Boni and Liveright, 1929.

Seims, Charles. *Mt. Lowe: Railway In The Clouds*. San Marino, CA: Golden West Books, 1976.

Smith, Jack. *Jack Smith's L. A.* New York: McGraw-Hill Company, 1980.

Smith, Sarah Bixby. *Adobe Days*. Los Angeles: J. Zeitlin, 1931.

Spalding, William A. *A History of Los Angeles City and County*. Vol. 1, Los Angeles: J. R. Finnell & Sons, 1931.

Starr, Kevin. *Material Dreams, Southern California Through the 1920s*. New York: Oxford University Press, 1990.

Warner, Jonathan T., Hayes Benjamin and Widney, Joseph P. *An Historical Sketch of Los Angeles County, California*. Los Angeles: Louis Lewin & Company, 1886.

SELECTED BIBLIOGRAPHY

Weaver, John W. *Los Angeles: The Enormous Village 1781-1981.* Santa Barbara: Capra Press, 1980.

Weber, Francis J. (Msgr.) *Angels Flight: A Los Angeles Funicular Railway.* Van Nuys, CA: Richard J. Hoffman (Printer), 1988.

Wheelock, Walt. *Angels Flight.* Glendale, CA: La Siesta Press, 1961.

Willard, Charles Dwight. *The Herald's History of Los Angeles City.* Los Angeles: Kingsley-Barnes & Neuner Co., 1901.

Wolfe, Wellington C. *Men of the Pacific Coast.* San Francisco: The Pacific Art Company, 1903.

Workman, Boyle. *The City That Grew: 1840-1936.* Los Angeles: The Southland Publishing Co., 1936.

INDEX

INDEX

INDEX

INDEX